THIRD EDITION

ESSENTIAL LIFE SKILLS SERIES

WHAT YOU NEED TO KNOW ABOUT

GETTING A JOB & FILLING OUT FORMS

Carolyn Morton Starkey

Norgina Wright Penn

National Textbook Company
NTC a division of *NTC Publishing Group* • Lincolnwood, Illinois USA

ACKNOWLEDGMENTS

Deluxe Check Printers, checks and deposit slips
McDonald's, job application form
Montgomery Ward & Co., credit application form
JC Penney, credit application
TOPS Business Forms, job application, telephone message form

Preface This third edition from the Essential Life Skills Series tells you what you need to know about getting a job and filling out forms. Mastering these skills will make you more assertive and self-confident. You will learn to cope better with everyday situations.

This book covers some familiar yet very important materials. You will learn to read, write, and understand:

job application letters	employment application forms
resumes	checks
job interviews	social security application
help-wanted ads	credit applications

Throughout the book you will find examples of real letters and memos, like the ones you see and use everyday.

Each section in this book includes definitions of words that may be new or difficult. Checkup sections help you review what you have learned. There are many opportunities to practice your skills. "Show What You Know" offers you the opportunity to apply your new skills.

Because of its flexible format, this book can be used either for self-study or in a group setting with an instructor. The answer key is on perforated pages so that it is easy to remove.

When you have mastered the skills in this book, you will want to develop other skills to become more successful in our modern world. The other books in the Essential Life Skills Series will show you how.

Essential Life Skills Series

What You Need to Know about Reading Labels, Directions & Newspapers 0-8442-5169-0

What You Need to Know about Reading Ads, Reference Materials & Legal Documents   0-8442-5170-4

What You Need to Know about Reading Signs, Directories, Schedules, Maps, Charts & Graphs   0-8442-5172-0

What You Need to Know about Basic Writing Skills, Letters & Consumer Complaints   0-8442-5173-9

Contents

Section 1 Getting a Job

Section 2 Filling Out Forms

Getting a job

Job-hunters need a lot of skills. This chapter outlines skills you need in your job search. Some skills you will need even before you begin your search. Other skills are needed during the search. And other skills are needed during the job interview. *Getting a Job* is divided into four job skill areas:

Fact Sheets, Resumes, and Application Letters
Job Application Forms
Job Interview Techniques
Telephone Communication Skills

First you will learn how to write clear, complete information about yourself. This will be in the form of a fact sheet, resume, and letter of application. Next you will learn to transfer this information to the job application. (A variety of job applications are included here.) How do you handle a job interview? How do you get information about a job over the phone? In this chapter you will learn job interview skills. And you will learn how the telephone can be an effective part of your job search.

Fact sheets, resumes, and application letters

WORDS TO KNOW

application   a form used for making a request, such as a job application or an application for credit

qualifications   a person's education and skills

references   a list of persons who know your work

resume   (rez'-e-mā) a description of education and work experience

Personal fact sheet

A fact sheet can be useful when you fill out job applications. Carry your personal fact sheet with you to provide names, dates, and numbers asked on application forms. There is no special form for a personal fact sheet. But it can look like the one on the next page. Study the sample. It gives facts about Nicarol Brown.

1

PERSONAL FACT SHEET

Name _Nicarol Brown_

Address _101 E. Maple Rd._   Phone # _555-8848_

Ronstead, CA 90901

Social Security # _521-06-9432_

Education
Schools Attended   Dates   Graduated   Diploma/Degree

Ronstead Elementary	_1977-1983_	_yes_	
Ronstead High School	_1983-1988_	_yes_	_Diploma_
Adams Community College	_1988-1991_	_yes_	_Certificate_

Work Experience
Employer   Address   Dates
                                                                  From   To

Ajax Manufacturing	_10 Main St., Ronstead, CA 90902_	_1991_	_Present_
Adams Community College	_851 North St., Canary, CA 90810_	_1989_	_1991_
Win's Pharmacy	_25 West Custer, Ronstead, CA 90901_	_1987_	_1989_

Special Interests or Skills

Computers — 2 courses in computer programming

Sports — soccer and softball

Music — member of high school band

Honors

Computer project award

References (other than members of the family)
Name   Address   Phone No.

Mary Fischer	_19 Willow Pl., Ronstead, CA 90901_	_555-1201_
Adam Johnson	_85 West Holiday, Ronstead, CA 90902_	_555-8106_
Lenore Bains	_182 Avery Pl., Canary, CA 90812_	_555-1604_

ACTIVITY 1
Making a personal fact sheet

Write your own personal fact sheet. Use the sample to help you.

Resumes

Many people apply for jobs by using resumes. A resume is a summary of your education and work experience. Your resume is important. It might be the one thing an employer has that describes *you*. Some job ads will say "send resume." Sometimes people who are looking for certain jobs will send out resumes. They want to know if a business or institution needs someone with their skills.

Resumes may be written in different ways. The type you write depends on what you want. If you are not applying for a specific job, you need to send a detailed resume. You want to know if there are any jobs that match your abilities. If you apply for a specific job, your resume should stress those skills that relate to that job. From time to time, you should update your resume.

A detailed resume

A detailed resume includes personal information and special interests. It also lists your educational background and job history. Special skills and references are also sections of a detailed resume. You might not need all of these sections. Employers who see many job requests each day may only want to see education and work background.

Below you will find the sections you *can* include in a detailed resume. Remember, it is always wise to write your resume to fit your own needs.

Personal Information:

At the top of the resume, put your name, address, and telephone number.

Special Interests:

Briefly list your special interests and achievements. You can include (1) places you have traveled, studied, or worked. (2) community or school achievement, (3) special hobbies, interests, or projects.

These two sections introduce you in a *personal* way. The rest of the resume should present you in a *professional* way.

Educational Background:

Give the name and location of each school you have attended. Give your major and minor, and the degree, certificate, or diploma (if any) you received. Give dates attended and your graduation date.

Employment History:

Starting with your present or most recent job, list the jobs you have held. Briefly describe your duties. If you have a good work record, include how long you worked at each job. If you have changed jobs often, you may want to leave out the dates. Include the name of your employer (e.g., Fine Foods Supermarket). Also include the address.

Special Skills:

List any special skills that you have obtained during your working career. Include·on-the-job training, supervising, or other special skills. Arrange

3

these so that the employer will quickly see what you can do. You can also put the length of time you have used a skill. (We have included just one way of doing this section in the sample resume that follows. You may want to add to it or take away parts.)

References: List the names of at least three people who can comment on your work abilities and personality. If you cannot include employers, list former teachers. You may also want to include community leaders. Give the names, addresses, telephone numbers, and job titles of these people.

RESUME

PERSONAL INFORMATION

Name: Clarence E. Smith
Address: 108 Mill Street
Bel Air, Maryland 21001
Phone Number: 301-555-0121

SPECIAL INTERESTS

I attended public schools in Bel Air, Maryland. My career interest since my sophomore year in high school has been in business. I participated in Bel Air High's Distributive Education Program my junior and senior years. The program combined school and work experience through various local businesses.

In high school I served two years as the president of the Minicorp Production Company, a Junior Achievement student business sponsored by the C&P Telephone Company. I was also a member of DECA—Distributive Education Clubs of America. When I graduated from Bel Air High School in 1991, I received an $800 scholarship from the local Chamber of Commerce. I was voted the "outstanding business student of the year." I am presently taking night courses in business at Harford Community College.

EDUCATIONAL BACKGROUND

Bel Air High School — Graduated 1991
Bel Air, Maryland
Course of Study: Distributive Education (Business Education)

Harford Community College — Attended Summer 1991–present
Aberdeen, Maryland
Major: Business Administration

EMPLOYMENT HISTORY

Employer: Quick Shop Mini Mart
Aberdeen, Maryland

Position: Stock person/cashier— I was in charge of pricing and stocking all merchandise for sale. This included creating sales displays and promotions for seasonal and holiday items. I also covered all register tours for employees absent or on vacation. I used the Sharp 3510 electronic cash register.

Employer: Baren's Furniture Store
Route 18
Bel Air, Maryland

Position: Floor Salesperson — As part of the Distributive Education Program at Bel Air High, I worked part time during school hours at Baren's Furniture. I averaged 20–25 hours per week as a furniture and appliance salesperson. I handled both cash and charge purchases. I operated a Martex 1050 register.

Employer: Burger Town
Town Center
Bel Air, Maryland

Position: Cashier — In this part-time assignment I gained fast-food experience. At this busy Town Center location, I worked both the "Drive-Thru" service and the regular "eat-in" customer service lines.

SPECIAL SKILLS

Type of Skill	Length of Experience	Job or Training Location
Operating electronic cash registers	3 years	Quick Shop Mini Mart Baren's Furniture Store Burger Town
Stocking	2 years	Quick Shop Mini Mart
Taking inventory	2 years	Quick Shop Mini Mart Baren's Furniture Store
Using office machines: calculators, adding machines, typewriters, etc.	2 years	Quick Shop Mini Mart Baren's Furniture Store
Using Vydec and Wang word processing machines, tele-typewriters, and office computers	1 semester	Harford Community College: Business Machines and Computer Programming

REFERENCES

Mary Wright, Manager
Quick Shop Mini Mart
Aberdeen, Maryland 21001
301-555-4583

Wilson Logan, Owner
Burger Town
Town Center
Bel Air, Maryland 21014
301-555-7983

Laverne Jackson
Supervisor of Distributive Education
Bel Air High School
Bel Air, Maryland 21014
301-555-9786

Regina Holmes, Assistant Manager
Baren's Furniture
Route 18
Bel Air, Maryland 21014
301-555-2933

ACTIVITY 2
Writing a detailed job resume

You have just seen a sample of Clarence Smith's detailed resume. Now write *your own* detailed resume. Make sure your resume has these sections:

- Personal Information
  - Name
  - Address
  - Phone No.

- Special Interests

- Educational Background

- Employment History

- Special Skills

- References

A brief resume

A brief resume should stress your skills for a specific job. It should have at least these four sections: (1) Position Applied For, (2) Experience, (3) Education, and (4) References. Below is a sample of a brief, one-page resume.

Thomas A. Lawson
27 DunbarStreet
Townsend, MO 64497
(417) 555-8904

POSITION APPLIED FOR: Accounting Clerk

EXPERIENCE:
June 1991 to
present

Accounts receivable clerk
Weston's Department Store, Townsend, MO
Duties: Posting and balancing accounts, preparing statements
Salary: Staring $175 Present $225

August 1989 to
June 1991

Stock clerk (part-time) Thompson's Department Store,
Townsend, MO
Duties: Organizing and pricing stock

Education:

High School Graduate, 1989, Townsend High School

Major Subjects: Accounting, Office Machines,
                       Business Mathematics, Business
                       Management

Grade Average: B

Extracurricular: President of Junior Class
                       Treasurer of Senior Class
                       President of Future Business
                           Leaders of America

REFERENCES:

Mr. Frank Marshall, Accounting Supervisor
Weston's Department Store
85 Mason Street
Townsend, MO 64497
(417) 555-7702

Ms. Francine Yamada, Manager
Thompson's Department Store
33 Basin Street
Townsend, MO 64497
(417) 555-9802

Mr. Ira Goldman, Advisor
FBLA Club
Townsend High School
92 Fairlane Drive
Townsend, MO 64497
(417) 555-5400

ACTIVITY 3
Writing a brief resume

Write a brief resume. Apply for any job you are qualified to do. See page 140 for the four parts of a brief resume.

Letters of application

Sometimes you may have to write a letter of application. It may be in response to a help-wanted ad. Or it may simply be part of your own job hunting efforts. Like the resume, the type of application letter you write will depend on the situation. If there are a number of people applying for the same job, you must write an especially effective letter.

The letter of application usually has the resume with it. The letter should contain three parts:

1. A statement of interest in a specific position
2. A brief statement of your abilities for this position (including a comment about your enclosed resume)
3. Information on how and where you can be reached

Remember:

- Try to obtain a *name* of a person. Write your letter of application to that person.

- Your letter should be typewritten and neat.

ACTIVITY 4
Understanding letters of application

Answer the questions about this letter of application.

126 Rockford Street
Chinaville, Ohio 44507
March 30, 19—

Mr. James Benawra
Personnel Director
The Superior Manufacturing Company
22 West Road
Merrytown, Ohio 44509

Dear Mr. Benawra:

Expression of interest in a particular position ● ——— Please consider this letter an application for a secretarial position in your main office.

Your qualifications ● —— I graduated from Malcolm X High School in June 1992, after completing a three-year secretarial course. My typing and shorthand speeds are 60 and 120 words per minute respectively.

A resume of my high school and previous work experience is enclosed. I have been employed as a part-time secretary for the past two years. If given the opportunity, I believe I would prove myself an asset to your company.

How and where you can be reached ● ——— I would appreciate the opportunity to talk with you at your convenience. I may be reached at the above address or by telephone (555-8181).

Very truly yours,

Alexander Brown

Alexander Brown

1. What type of position is Alexander applying for? ————————————————

——

2. What is the position of the person Alexander is writing to? ————————

——

3. What are Alexander's qualifications? ————————————————————

——

4. What is Alexander asking for as a result of his letter? ————————————

——

5. How can he be reached? ———————————————————————————

——

6. What will Alexander include with his letter of application? ——————————

7. What previous work experience does he mention? ———————————————

8. Did Alexander graduate from high school?————— If so, name the school. ——————

9. What is Alexander's typing speed? ————————————————————————

10. What is Alexander's home address? ————————————————————————

9

On your own paper, write a letter of application. Select a job you might be interested in now or in the future.

SHOW WHAT YOU KNOW . . .

About Letters of Application

Find four help-wanted ads in your local newspaper. Look for jobs that interest you. After studying the ads carefully, choose two of them to answer. Write a letter of application for each. Be sure that your letters mention the particular position given in the ad.

Job application forms

Nearly every job requires some form of written application. Most job applications have similar sections: personal information, education, work history, and references. Some applications, however, will have other sections, such as physical record, military service, and special skills. The job application should be completed correctly and neatly. Like the resume, it may be the only thing that tells an employer about you.

ACTIVITY 5
Filling out job applications

Study the following completed application and answer the questions about it.

APPLICATION FOR EMPLOYMENT

(PRE-EMPLOYMENT QUESTIONNAIRE)   (AN EQUAL OPPORTUNITY EMPLOYER)

Date __July 17, 19—__

Name [Last Name First] __Johnson, Michael L.__   Soc. Sec. No. __621-01-8841__

Address __422 Asbury Dr., Los Angeles, CA 90032__   Telephone __555-6113__

What kind of work are you applying for? __stock worker__

What special qualifications do you have? __strong, reliable__

What office machines can you operate? __typewriter__

Are you 18 years or older?   Yes __X__   No _____

SPECIAL PURPOSE QUESTIONS

DO NOT ANSWER **ANY** OF THE QUESTIONS IN THIS FRAMED AREA UNLESS THE EMPLOYER HAS **CHECKED A BOX PRECEDING** A QUESTION, THEREBY INDICATING THAT THE INFORMATION IS REQUIRED FOR A BONA FIDE OCCUPATIONAL QUALIFICATION, OR DICTATED BY NATIONAL SECURITY LAWS, OR IS NEEDED FOR OTHER LEGALLY PERMISSIBLE REASONS.

☐ HEIGHT _____ FEET _____ INCHES _____   ☐ WEIGHT _____ LBS.   ☐ CITIZEN OF U.S.   YES _____ NO _____

☐ _____

MILITARY SERVICE RECORD

Armed Forces Service _____ Yes _____ No _____   From* _____   To* _____

Branch of Service _____   Duties _____

Rank or rating at time of enlistment _____   Rating at time of discharge _____

Do you have any physical limitations that prohibit you from performing any work for which you are being considered?   Yes _____ No _____ . Please describe. _____

EDUCATION

SCHOOL	*NO. OF YEARS ATTENDED	NAME OF SCHOOL	CITY	COURSE	*DID YOU GRADUATE?
GRAMMAR					
HIGH	4	L.A. High School	Los Angeles	vocational	yes
COLLEGE					
OTHER					

*The Age Discrimination in Employment Act of 1967 prohibits discrimination on the basis of age with respect to individuals who are at least 40 but less than 70 years of age.

EXPERIENCE

NAME AND ADDRESS OF COMPANY	DATE FROM	DATE TO	LIST YOUR DUTIES	STARTING SALARY	FINAL SALARY	REASON FOR LEAVING
Lynn's Apparel	1991	1993	preparing stock	$4.35	$5.60	need full time

BUSINESS REFERENCES

NAME	ADDRESS	OCCUPATION
Mr. Ted Anderson	Lynn's Apparel, 14921 Commons Pl.	store manager

1. What position does Michael want? _____

2. Which high school did he attend? _____

3. What was his high school course of study? _____

4. Has Michael attended a college or trade school? _____

5. Can he operate any special machines or equipment? If so, which? _____

6. What kind of job has he had before? _____

7. Does Michael want to work full time or part time? _____

8. Has Michael served in the armed forces? _____

9. Does Michael need to tell this employer how tall he is? _____

10. Did Michael give his weight?_____ Why or why not? _____

ACTIVITY 6
Understanding a job application form

The following application is divided into sections. Each section contains step-by-step directions. Read and study these directions before completing this application.

APPLICATION FOR EMPLOYMENT
(PRE-EMPLOYMENT QUESTIONNAIRE)   (AN EQUAL OPPORTUNITY EMPLOYER)

PERSONAL INFORMATION

(1) DATE _____

(2) NAME _____
   LAST   FIRST   MIDDLE

SOCIAL SECURITY NUMBER

(3) PRESENT ADDRESS _____
            STREET   CITY   STATE

(4) PERMANENT ADDRESS _____
            STREET   CITY   STATE

(5) PHONE NO. _____   ARE YOU 18 YEARS OR OLDER   Yes ☐   No ☐

---

(1) Print today's date.

(2) Print your last name, then first name, then middle name or initial. Clearly print your social security number.

(3) Print your present address. Be sure to include your ZIP Code.

(4) If your present address is temporary (such as a summer location), write your regular address here. If your present and permanent address are the same, print "Same" here.

(5) Clearly print the phone number where you can be reached.

EMPLOYMENT DESIRED

(6) POSITION _____ DATE YOU CAN START _____ SALARY DESIRED _____

(7) ARE YOU EMPLOYED NOW? _____ IF SO MAY WE INQUIRE OF YOUR PRESENT EMPLOYER? _____

(8) EVER APPLIED TO THIS COMPANY BEFORE? _____ WHERE? _____ WHEN? _____

---

(6) List the job you are asking for, when you can start, and what pay you expect.

(7) Print "Yes" if you are working now and "No" if you are not. They are asking your permission to ask your employer about your work ability.

(8) If you have applied there before, they want to know the location and dates you applied. This is used to locate any records they may have on you.

---

(9) EDUCATION	NAME AND LOCATION OF SCHOOL	*NO. OF YEARS ATTENDED	*DID YOU GRADUATE?	SUBJECTS STUDIED
GRAMMAR SCHOOL				
HIGH SCHOOL				
COLLEGE				
TRADE, BUSINESS OR CORRESPONDENCE SCHOOL				

---

(9) Name the schools you attended, the years you attended, when you graduated, and the main subjects you studied.

(10) SUBJECTS OF SPECIAL STUDY OR RESEARCH WORK

(11) U.S. MILITARY OR NAVAL SERVICE	RANK

PRESENT MEMBERSHIP IN NATIONAL GUARD OR RESERVES

(12) Activities—civic. athletic. fraternal. etc.
(exclude organizations which indicate race. religion, color or national origin of members)

(10) Name any special subject you have studied.

(11) Name, if any, the branch of service you have been in and the rank you obtained. Indicate whether you are presently a member of the National Guard or Reserves.

(12) If you are active in any club, write it here. *Do not* write the name of a club that would indicate your race, beliefs, or national origin.

(13) FORMER EMPLOYERS [LIST BELOW LAST FOUR EMPLOYERS. STARTING WITH LAST ONE FIRST].

DATE MONTH AND YEAR	NAME AND ADDRESS OF EMPLOYER	SALARY	POSITION	REASON FOR LEAVING
FROM				
TO				
FROM				
TO				
FROM				
TO				
FROM				
TO				

(13) Starting with your last job, name the company you worked for and give its address. List what you were paid, the position you held, and your reason for leaving.

(14) REFERENCES: GIVE THE NAMES OF THREE PERSONS NOT RELATED TO YOU, WHOM YOU HAVE KNOWN AT LEAST ONE YEAR.

	NAME	ADDRESS	BUSINESS	YEARS ACQUAINTED
1				
2				
3				

(14) Name three adults who can say what type of worker you are. Be sure to include full addresses and how long you have known each.

PHYSICAL RECORD:

(15) DO YOU HAVE ANY PHYSICAL LIMITATIONS THAT PRECLUDE YOU FROM PERFORMING ANY WORK FOR WHICH YOU ARE BEING CONSIDERED? ☐ Yes ☐ No

PLEASE DESCRIBE: _____

_____

(16) IN CASE OF
EMERGENCY NOTIFY

(17)

NAME	ADDRESS	PHONE NO.

"I CERTIFY THAT THE FACTS CONTAINED IN THIS APPLICATION ARE TRUE AND COMPLETE TO THE BEST OF MY KNOWLEDGE AND UNDERSTAND THAT, IF EMPLOYED, FALSIFIED STATEMENTS ON THIS APPLICATION SHALL BE GROUNDS FOR DISMISSAL.

I AUTHORIZE INVESTIGATION OF ALL STATEMENTS CONTAINED HEREIN AND THE REFERENCES LISTED ABOVE TO GIVE YOU ANY AND ALL INFORMATION CONCERNING MY PREVIOUS EMPLOYMENT AND ANY PERTINENT INFORMATION THEY MAY HAVE, PERSONAL OR OTHERWISE, AND RELEASE ALL PARTIES FROM ALL LIABILITY FOR ANY DAMAGE THAT MAY RESULT FROM FURNISHING SAME TO YOU.

I UNDERSTAND AND AGREE THAT, IF HIRED, MY EMPLOYMENT IS FOR NO DEFINITE PERIOD AND MAY, REGARDLESS OF THE DATE OF PAYMENT OF MY WAGES AND SALARY, BE TERMINATED AT ANY TIME WITHOUT ANY PRIOR NOTICE."

(18) DATE   SIGNATURE

---

(15) Describe any major injuries or handicap that you may have.

(16) Name someone who should be reached if something happens to you on the job. The address and telephone number are very important.

(17) This is a statement written *for you*. It reads as if you wrote it. You are giving the company permission

    (a) to check on any facts you have put on this application.
    (b) to dismiss (fire) you if they find any of your statements false.
    (c) to dismiss you at any time without giving you notice.

(18) Use today's date and sign (write out) your name.

ACTIVITY 7
Filling out job applications

Following are two job application forms. Complete each form for practice. Use today's date. Select any position that interests you now or may in the future. The first form is for McDonald's, and the second is a general job application.

    The back of the McDonald's application contains a federal Form W-4. For tax purposes, every employer is required by law to obtain the information listed on the Form W-4. If you work, be sure to have a Form W-4 on file with your employer.

EMPLOYMENT APPLICATION

SOCIAL SECURITY NO. _____

NAME _____
FIRST NAME _____ MIDDLE INITIAL _____ LAST NAME _____

APT. NO.
OR BOX _____
_____ CITY _____ STATE _____ ZIP _____ STREET ADDRESS _____
AREA CODE _____ TEL. NO. _____

ARE YOU 18
OR OLDER? ☐ YES ☐ NO, IF NOT, AGE _____

EVER WORKED IN A McDONALD'S RESTAURANT BEFORE?
IF YES, DATES, LOCATION AND REASON FOR LEAVING _____

AVAILABILITY:

TOTAL HOURS AVAILABLE PER WEEK _____

	M	T	W	T	F	S	S
HOURS AVAILABLE: FROM							
TO							

ARE YOU LEGALLY ABLE TO
BE EMPLOYED IN THE U.S.: ☐ YES ☐ NO

HOW DID YOU
HEAR OF JOB? _____

HOW FAR DO YOU
LIVE FROM RESTAURANT? _____

DO YOU HAVE
TRANSPORTATION TO WORK? _____

SCHOOL MOST RECENTLY ATTENDED:

NAME _____ LOCATION _____

TEACHER OR
COUNSELOR _____ DEPT. _____ PHONE _____

GRADUATED ☐ YES ☐ NO   NOW ENROLLED? ☐ YES ☐ NO

SPORTS OR
ACTIVITIES _____

LAST GRADE
COMPLETED _____

GRADE
POINT AVERAGE _____

TWO MOST RECENT JOBS: (IF NOT APPLICABLE, LIST U.S. MILITARY, WORK PERFORMED ON A VOLUNTARY BASIS OR PERSONAL REFERENCES)

SALARY _____ REASON FOR LEAVING _____

SUPERVISOR _____

PHONE _____ JOB _____

COMPANY _____ LOCATION _____ DATES WORKED: FROM _____ TO _____

MGMT. REFERENCE CHECK DONE BY

SALARY _____ REASON FOR LEAVING _____

SUPERVISOR _____

PHONE _____ JOB _____

COMPANY _____ LOCATION _____ DATES WORKED: FROM _____ TO _____

MGMT. REFERENCE CHECK DONE BY

* DURING THE PAST 7 YEARS, HAVE YOU EVER BEEN CONVICTED OF A CRIME, EXCLUDING MISDEMEANORS AND TRAFFIC VIOLATIONS?
☐ YES ☐ NO . IF YES, DESCRIBE IN FULL _____

* A conviction will not necessarily bar you from employment.

1. I certify that the information contained in this application is correct to the best of my knowledge and understand that any omission or erroneous information is grounds for dismissal in accordance with McDonald's policy. 2. I authorize the references listed above to give you any and all information concerning my previous employment and pertinent information they may have, personal or otherwise, and release all parties from all liability for any damage that may result from furnishing same to you. 3. I acknowledge that McDonald's reserves the right to amend or modify the policies in its Handbook and other McDonald's policies at any time, without prior notice. These policies do not create any promises or contractual obligations between McDonald's and its employees. At McDonald's, my employment is at will. This means I am free to terminate my employment at any time, for any reason, with or without cause, and McDonald's retains the same rights. The Senior Vice President of Personnel of the Corporation is the only person who may make an exception to this, and it must be in writing and signed by him.   DATE _____   SIGNATURE _____

NOTE: Employees working in **Massachusetts**—see reverse side for important information.

The Secretary of Health and Human Services has determined that certain diseases, including **hepatitis A, salmonella, shigella, staphylococcus, streptococcus, giardia and compylobacter** may prevent you from serving food or handling food equipment in a sanitary or healthy fashion. An essential function of this job involves handling and serving food, food service equipment and utensils in a sanitary and healthy fashion. Is there any reason why you cannot perform the essential functions of this job? ☐ YES ☐ NO   If yes, explain: _____

YOUR APPLICATION WILL BE CONSIDERED ACTIVE FOR 30 DAYS - FOR CONSIDERATION AFTER THAT YOU MUST REAPPLY.

Printed on Recycled Paper

OB PRODUCT NO. 4850125 (REV. 2/93) McOpCo

O'BRIEN BUDD, INC. 1-800-762-7430

Form W-4

Department of the Treasury
Internal Revenue Service

Employee's Withholding Allowance Certificate

▶ For Privacy Act and Paperwork Reduction Act Notice, see reverse.

OMB No. 1545-0010

1993

1 Type or print your first name and middle initial | Last name | **2** Your social security number

Home address (number and street or rural route)

City or town, state, and ZIP code

3 Marital status
- ☐ Single ☐ Married
- ☐ Married, but withhold at higher Single rate.

Note: *If married, but legally separated, or spouse is a nonresident alien, check the Single box.*

4 Total number of allowances you are claiming (from line G above or from the Worksheets on back if they apply) . . . . ▶ | **4** |

5 Additional amount, if any, you want deducted from each pay . . . . | **5** | $

6 I claim exemption from withholding and I certify that I meet ALL of the following conditions for exemption:
- Last year I had a right to a refund of ALL Federal income tax withheld because I had NO tax liability; AND
- This year I expect a refund of ALL Federal income tax withheld because I expect to have NO tax liability; AND
- This year if my income exceeds $500 and includes nonwage income, another person cannot claim me as a dependent.

If you meet all of the above conditions, enter the year effective and "EXEMPT" here . . . . . . ▶ | **6** | 19

7 Are you a full-time student? (Note: *Full-time students are not automatically exempt.*) | **7** ☐ Yes ☐ No

Under penalties of perjury, I certify that I am entitled to the number of withholding allowances claimed on this certificate or entitled to claim exempt status

Employee's signature ▶ | Date ▶ | , 19

8 Employer's name and address (Employer: Complete 8 and 10 only if sending to IRS) | **9** Office code (optional) | **10** Employer identification number

---

IF YOU WANT THE COMPLETE W4 WITH INSTRUCTIONS, PLEASE ASK THE RESTAURANT MANAGER.

W4 IS TO BE FILLED OUT ONLY AFTER HIRE.

TO MASSACHUSETTS EMPLOYEES:

An applicant for employment with a sealed record on file with the commissioner of probation may answer 'no record' with respect to any inquiry herein relative to prior arrests, criminal court appearances or convictions. An applicant for employment with a sealed record on file with the commissioner of probation may answer 'no record' to an inquiry herein relative to prior arrests or criminal court appearances. In addition, any applicant for employment may answer 'no record' with respect to any inquiry relative to prior arrests, court appearances and adjudications in all cases of delinquency or as a child in need of services which did not result in a complaint transferred to the superior court for criminal prosecution.

It is unlawful in Massachusetts to require or administer a lie detector test as a condition of employment or continued employment. An employer who violates this law shall be subject to criminal penalties and civil liabilities.

APPLICATION FOR EMPLOYMENT
(PRE-EMPLOYMENT QUESTIONNAIRE) (AN EQUAL OPPORTUNITY EMPLOYER)

PERSONAL INFORMATION

DATE _____

SOCIAL SECURITY
NUMBER _____

NAME _____
LAST   FIRST   MIDDLE

PRESENT ADDRESS _____
STREET   CITY   STATE   ZIP

PERMANENT ADDRESS _____
STREET   CITY   STATE   ZIP

PHONE NO. _____   ARE YOU 18 YEARS OR OLDER? Yes ☐ No ☐

ARE YOU EITHER A U.S. CITIZEN OR AN ALIEN AUTHORIZED TO WORK IN THE UNITED STATES?   Yes ☐ No ☐

EMPLOYMENT DESIRED

POSITION _____   DATE YOU CAN START _____   SALARY DESIRED _____

ARE YOU EMPLOYED NOW? _____   IF SO MAY WE INQUIRE OF YOUR PRESENT EMPLOYER? _____

EVER APPLIED TO THIS COMPANY BEFORE? _____   WHERE? _____   WHEN? _____

REFERRED BY _____

EDUCATION	NAME AND LOCATION OF SCHOOL	*NO OF YEARS ATTENDED	*DID YOU GRADUATE?	SUBJECTS STUDIED
GRAMMAR SCHOOL				
HIGH SCHOOL				
COLLEGE				
TRADE, BUSINESS OR CORRESPONDENCE SCHOOL				

GENERAL
SUBJECTS OF SPECIAL STUDY OR RESEARCH WORK _____

SPECIAL SKILLS _____

ACTIVITIES: (CIVIC, ATHLETIC, ETC.) _____
EXCLUDE ORGANIZATIONS, THE NAME OF WHICH INDICATES THE RACE, CREED, SEX, AGE, MARITAL STATUS, COLOR OR NATION OF ORIGIN OF ITS MEMBERS.

U.S. MILITARY OR NAVAL SERVICE _____   RANK _____   PRESENT MEMBERSHIP IN NATIONAL GUARD OR RESERVES _____

*The Age Discrimination in Employment Act of 1987 prohibits discrimination on the basis of age with respect to individuals who are at least 40 years of age.

LAST

FIRST

MIDDLE

TOPS FORM 3285 (89-8)   (CONTINUED ON OTHER SIDE)   LITHO IN U.S.A.

FORMER EMPLOYERS (LIST BELOW LAST THREE EMPLOYERS, STARTING WITH LAST ONE FIRST).

DATE MONTH AND YEAR	NAME AND ADDRESS OF EMPLOYER	SALARY	POSITION	REASON FOR LEAVING
FROM				
TO				
FROM				
TO				
FROM				
TO				
FROM				
TO				

WHICH OF THESE JOBS DID YOU LIKE BEST?

WHAT DID YOU LIKE MOST ABOUT THIS JOB?

REFERENCES: GIVE THE NAMES OF THREE PERSONS NOT RELATED TO YOU, WHOM YOU HAVE KNOWN AT LEAST ONE YEAR.

	NAME	ADDRESS	BUSINESS	YEARS ACQUAINTED
1				
2				
3				

THE FOLLOWING STATEMENT APPLIES IN: MARYLAND & MASSACHUSETTS. (Fill in name of state)
IT IS UNLAWFUL IN THE STATE OF _____ TO REQUIRE OR ADMINISTER A LIE DETECTOR TEST AS A
CONDITION OF EMPLOYMENT OR CONTINUED EMPLOYMENT. AN EMPLOYER WHO VIOLATES THIS LAW SHALL BE
SUBJECT TO CRIMINAL PENALTIES AND CIVIL LIABILITY.

Signature of Applicant

IN CASE OF
EMERGENCY NOTIFY

NAME	ADDRESS	PHONE NO.

"I CERTIFY THAT THE FACTS CONTAINED IN THIS APPLICATION ARE TRUE AND COMPLETE TO THE BEST OF MY KNOWLEDGE AND
UNDERSTAND THAT, IF EMPLOYED, FALSIFIED STATEMENTS ON THIS APPLICATION SHALL BE GROUNDS FOR DISMISSAL.

I AUTHORIZE INVESTIGATION OF ALL STATEMENTS CONTAINED HEREIN AND THE REFERENCES LISTED ABOVE TO GIVE YOU ANY
AND ALL INFORMATION CONCERNING MY PREVIOUS EMPLOYMENT AND ANY PERTINENT INFORMATION THEY MAY HAVE, AND RE-
LEASE ALL PARTIES FROM ALL LIABILITY FOR ANY DAMAGE THAT MAY RESULT FROM FURNISHING SAME TO YOU.

I UNDERSTAND AND AGREE THAT, IF HIRED, MY EMPLOYMENT IS FOR NO DEFINITE PERIOD AND MAY, REGARDLESS OF THE DATE
OF PAYMENT OF MY WAGES AND SALARY, BE TERMINATED AT ANY TIME WITHOUT PRIOR NOTICE AND WITHOUT CAUSE."

DATE   SIGNATURE

DO NOT WRITE BELOW THIS LINE

INTERVIEWED BY   DATE

REMARKS:

NEATNESS   ABILITY

HIRED: ☐ Yes ☐ No   POSITION   DEPT.

SALARY/WAGE   DATE REPORTING TO WORK

APPROVED: 1. _____ 2. _____ 3. _____
EMPLOYMENT MANAGER   DEPT. HEAD   GENERAL MANAGER

Answer the following questions about job application forms.

1. What is your social security number? _____

2. If you have had three jobs, which one do you list first on a job application form? _____

3. What is an equal opportunity employer? _____

4. Which of the following pieces of information should you leave off an application for a job as a mail-room clerk? _____

   a. permanent address   **b.** telephone number
   c. church membership   **d.** military service

5. What is the difference between a present address and a permanent address?

   _____

6. What is a "bona fide occupational qualification"? _____

7. Some job applications, such as the one shown here, state that "employment . . . may be terminated at any time without prior notice and without cause."

   What does this mean? _____

8. Many employers use application forms that indicate they are equal opportunity employers. What does this mean? According to the statement on the application shown here, what is one specific factor that a prospective employer cannot legally consider when hiring a new employee?

9. Suppose you are filling out a job application form at the personnel office of Ace Office Machine Co. You discover that you have written your name in ink on the wrong line of the form. Would you ask the secretary for another form? Why or why not?

   _____

10. Name three major types or sections of information asked on job application forms.

   _____

SHOW WHAT YOU KNOW . . .

About Job Application Forms

Obtain at least one job application form from a local employer. Complete the application, using what you have learned in this chapter.

Job interview techniques

Several people may be right for a job. That is why your interview skills are so important. They may be what gets you the job! There are several points you should think about when getting ready for the job interview.

Before the Interview:

1. *Go over your school record.* Know what subjects you had in school and which ones relate to the job you want. Be able to list your school activities, honors, hobbies, and your grade average and attendance record.
2. *Understand the job you are applying for.* Learn about the duties of the job.
3. *Pay special attention to your appearance.* Select clothes that are neat, clean, comfortable, and proper. Be sure that you are well rested and well groomed.
4. *Be on time!* Being on time is important on any job. Being late for the interview makes a very poor impression.

During the Interview:

1. *Be polite.* Listen carefully to what the interviewer has to say. Do not interrupt. Thank the interviewer for time and interest spent.
2. *Use your best speaking manner.* Speak clearly. Answer questions with confidence. Be brief and exact. Avoid long answers, but say enough to answer questions.
3. *Follow the interviewer's lead.* The interviewer will probably tell you about the salary and working hours. Showing too much interest in lunch time, vacation time, sick leave, or short working hours may give the impression that you are more interested in time off than the time on.

ACTIVITY 8
Preparing for a job interview

Use the checklist below to rate yourself on how prepared you are for a job interview. This is practice now, but you may save this checklist to use when you prepare for a real job interview.

Name _____

Job Interview Considerations	Yes ✓	Needs More Work ✓
1. I am familiar with my qualifications.		
2. I understand the job I am applying for.		
3. I know proper grooming and dress.		
4. I am on time for appointments.		
5. I am courteous.		
6. I have a good speaking manner.		
7. I am able to answer questions directly.		
8. I do not smoke or chew gum during the interview.		

ACTIVITY 9
Preparing for a job interview

Below are some usual interview questions and responses. Some of the responses might hurt the applicant's chances of getting a job. Do you think the interviewer will *like* or *dislike* these responses? Code each response as L (like) or D (dislike). Explain each of your choices.

Interviewer's Question	Applicant's Response	L	D	Explain
1. "Why did you apply to our company?"	"Because I live close to here."	___	___	_____ _____
2. "Why did you leave your last job?"	"I couldn't get along with my boss."	___	___	_____ _____

3. "Are you willing to work overtime?"	"It depends on which days. I play softball on Tuesdays and Thursdays."	_____ _____ _____ _____
4. "Why are you applying for this job?"	"Because I need a job."	_____ _____ _____ _____
5. "When can you start?"	"Not until next week. I want to get a little more tennis practice in before it gets too hot."	_____ _____ _____ _____

ACTIVITY 10
Preparing for a job interview

Your ability to communicate well in a job interview is important. Often *how* you say something can decide an interviewer's reaction. Did you say enough to answer questions completely? Did you say too much? Did you say something that will hurt your chances of getting a job? Did your need for better language skills prevent you from saying what you meant? Select the *best* response for each of the questions below.

_____ 1. "When can you start work?"
   (a) "Anytime next week."
   (b) "Will next week be okay with you?"
   (c) "Although I prefer Monday, I can start now, if you would like me to."

_____ 2. "Can you give me one or two references?"
   (a) "One of my teachers, I guess."
   (b) "You can talk to the manager at Sun Ray Cleaners or my teachers."
   (c) "You can contact Miss Anne Willis, my high school English teacher, and Mr. Randy Campos, the manager at Sun Ray Cleaners, where I worked last summer."

_____ 3. "Why did you leave your last job?"
   (a) "I wasn't learning nothing, and I never was going to get ahead."
   (b) "I couldn't get along with those people. They didn't show you how to do the job."
   (c) "I wanted to find a company that offered opportunities for advancement and training for its *new* employees."

_____ 4. "I noticed on your application that you live all the way across town. Will you have any difficulty getting to work?"
   (a) "Yeah. That's why I started not to come here."
   (b) "Well, this morning I caught a ride with a friend. It really is difficult to get a ride out this far."
   (c) "I've already considered that. And I can make arrangements to get to work every day, on time."

5. "On your application you indicate that you have cashier experience. What can you tell me about your experience?"
   (a) "Ain't nothing to tell. I just used the register."
   (b) "I operated the Accu-Count XL3 register while working at Barclay's Department store as a cashier."
   (c) "I worked the register at Barclay's."

6. "We were expecting you at 9:00 and you arrived at 9:30. Did you have any trouble finding us?"
   (a) "No, I didn't have any trouble."
   (b) "Finding you wasn't the problem. Getting up was the problem. My alarm clock didn't go off."
   (c) "I hope my being late has not inconvenienced you. The delay was unavoidable."

7. "Why did you decide to try our company?"
   (a) "I don't know. . . . I'm just trying everybody."
   (b) "In today's tough job market, a person has to try every company with an opening that matches his or her qualifications and experience."
   (c) "I couldn't leave a stone unturned."

8. "Why did you decide to take a job while still in school?"
   (a) "There're some things I want to do, and a job will make it a lot easier."
   (b) "My mother said find a job . . . so here I am."
   (c) "I'm old enough now to work a part-time job after school, and my family could really use the extra income."

Read each of the statements. Decide if each is TRUE (T) or FALSE (F).

_____ **1.** It is OK to chew gum during a job interview.

_____ **2.** It is not a good idea to wear blue jeans to a job interview.

_____ **3.** It is not necessary to prepare for an interview.

_____ **4.** It is all right to interrupt an interviewer.

_____ **5.** You will not be asked your school grade point average at an interview because that is private information.

Rewrite the following statements made during job interviews. Change them to improve the impression the applicant will make on the interviewer. You may want to model your answers after the best responses in Activity 10.

6. "I left my last job because I couldn't get along with my boss."

_____

_____

7. "I won't have no trouble getting to work because my sister's boyfriend works two miles from here, and he can bring me."

_____

_____

8. "I was late for the interview because my alarm didn't go off this morning."

_____

_____

9. "I quit my last job because I had a fight with another person who worked there."

_____

_____

10. "I came to this company because I need a job."

_____

_____

SHOW WHAT YOU KNOW . . .

About Job Interviews

You and a partner may use the situations below to role-play job interviewing. One of you act as the interviewer, and the other one act as the applicant. Select at least two situations for practice.

1. You are applying to be a salesclerk at a local department store.

2. You are applying to work in the stockroom at a local department store.

3. You are applying to be a counter person in a local burger place.

4. You are applying to be a bus person in a local restaurant.

5. You are applying to be an office helper at a local business.

Telephone communications skills

> ### WORDS TO KNOW
>
> **appropriate question**   a question that is proper for the situation
>
> **concise message**   a message that is short, complete, and clear
>
> **goal**   your aim or objective; what you wish to achieve
>
> **initial a memo**   to sign a short note with your initials
>
> **memo**   a brief note
>
> **receptionist**   a person whose job is to greet people
>
> **screen a caller for a job**   to save interview time by asking questions. If the caller does not meet certain needs, no interview is set up.
>
> **telephone dialogue**   a telephone talk between two people

It is important to know how to inquire about a job by phone. You may get an interview based on how well you handle a telephone call. Often help-wanted ads will tell you to call about the job advertised. You need to know how to take clear, complete phone messages while on the job, too. Good telephone skills can be an important part of getting and keeping a job.

Job hunting and telephone interview skills

Have you ever used the classified-ad section of the newspaper to find a job? You may know that many help-wanted ads ask you to call about the opening. Sometimes the name and address of the company are in the ad. Sometimes they aren't. Many employers do not have the space or staff to see many applicants. When you call about an ad, these employers screen you. They ask you questions to see if you should come in for an interview. Employers may ask if you have a driver's license. They may ask if you own a car. They will want to know how much experience you have. They may ask how far you live from the job. Your call will also tell you if a job is still open. Many jobs are filled soon after they appear in the paper.

Some ads give you specific job information. They list hours, pay, location, and qualifications. When employers run these ads, they expect *you* to screen yourself. The call you make should only be to find out *how* to apply: whom to see, where to go, and what time. Your phone interview should be brief. Your goal is simply to find out what to do to get this job.

There are times, however, when an ad does not tell enough about a job. This may be on purpose. If you have questions, you must ask them with caution. Some employers receive many calls each day. The only way they will give you information is to have you come in. To ask too many questions can only annoy the employer. Read job ads carefully. Decide *before* you call which questions are proper and which are not. If the employer has given you information in the ad, know that information. Don't ask for the location when it's already given. Plan your questions before the call, especially the *first* question. And follow the flow of the conversation. Sometimes, employers will volunteer information. George Jennings called Bilko Manufacturing about a plant job. The phone conversation appears below:

INTERVIEWER: "Bilko Manufacturing. Personnel Department."

GEORGE: "Do you still have openings for plant workers?"

INTERVIEWER: "Yes, we have several left. The night shift pays $6.35 per hour. The day shift pays $5.20. If you would like to apply, you can come into our personnel office from 9–4, Mondays through Fridays."

GEORGE: "Thank you."

If the person on the phone sounds rushed, you must cooperate. If the person insists that you set up an interview, then set it up.

PERSONNEL INTERVIEWER: "Johnson Book Distributors."

APPLICANT: "Do you still have openings for book packers?"

PERSONNEL INTERVIEWER: "Yes, we do. If you want to apply, you must come in to our personnel office. Interviews are being held tomorrow between 8 A.M. and 2 P.M."

APPLICANT: "What working hours are available?"

PERSONNEL INTERVIEWER: (*sounding annoyed*) "I'm sorry, I'm unable to discuss work hours or pay rates over the phone. If you're interested, you *must* come in tomorrow between 8 and 2."

APPLICANT: "Where are you located?"

PERSONNEL INTERVIEWER: "We're at 1581 Grand Boulevard East. We're across from Worldwide Manufacturers. The personnel office is on the first floor" (telephone click).

APPLICANT: "Thank you."

Let's hope this applicant got the address and hours. A second call would annoy this interviewer. And the whole experience may have discouraged the job applicant. In this phone interview, a pencil and paper would have come in handy. It's always good to write down information you will need later. You should also circle the job ad you're interested in. You may need to look at the ad when you call about the job.

ACTIVITY 11
Telephoning about a job

Below you will find some job ads. There are also questions an applicant might ask. Some of these questions are proper over the phone. Others are not. In this activity you will decide which questions are suitable or proper and which are not.

```
WANTED
HIGH SCHOOL STUDENTS
FOR SUMMER WORK
CALL 555-7013
for information
```

• Which of these questions are suitable on the phone? Which are not? Explain your answers.

	Suitable (✓)	Unsuitable (X)	Explain
"Do you *have* to be in high school to get this job?"	_____	_____	_____
			_____
			_____
			_____
"Can you give me any information about the job over the phone?"	_____	_____	_____
			_____
			_____
"How can I find out more about the job for summer work you advertised in today's paper?"	_____	_____	_____
			_____
			_____

```
TUTORS NEEDED
Teenagers and adults.
Area high schools.
Nights. Help adults with
English, basic math, and
reading. Call: 555-6130
Ext. 481
```

- Which of these questions are suitable over the phone? Which are not? Explain your answers.

	Suitable (✓)	Unsuitable (X)	Explain
(After reaching ext. 481) "To whom may I talk to find out more about the openings for tutors advertised in today's (name of newspaper)?"	_____	_____	_____
(After reaching ext. 481) "How much do the tutor positions pay?"	_____	_____	_____
(After reaching ext. 481) "Are there any day openings? I don't really want to work nights."	_____	_____	_____
(Reaching switchboard) "I'd like to come in and apply for the job of tutor. Can you help me?"	_____	_____	_____
(Reaching switchboard) "Will you connect me with extension 481, please?"	_____	_____	_____

ACTIVITY 12
Evaluating telephone interviews

Below are several job ads. The applicant's *goals* are also stated. First, you are to read each ad. Then read the telephone conversation that follows the ad. Decide how the phone interview went. Did the applicant accomplish his or her goal?

Counselors Wanted
Summer day camps. Must
be 17 years or older. Some
day camp experience helpful
or experience with children
as day care aide, tutor, YMCA
worker, etc. Call Camping Inc.
555-1703, Ext.43

Applicant's goals:

1. To find out if there are still openings.

2. To try to determine if the job pays above the minimum wage before spending money to go across town for the interview.

APPLICANT: "Extension 43, please."

BOB MORRISON: "Bob Morrison."

APPLICANT: "I'm calling about your ad in the *Daily News* for day camp counselors."

BOB MORRISON: "Just a minute. I'll connect you with someone who can help you."

INTERVIEWER: "Hello. This is Anne Richardson. May I help you?"

APPLICANT: "Yes. It's about the counseling job . . ."

INTERVIEWER: (silence)

APPLICANT: "I'm interested in the job you advertised in the paper." (long pause . . . no response) "Do you still have positions available?"

INTERVIEWER: "Yes, we do. When can you come in for an interview?"

APPLICANT: "Well, I'd like to know how much the job pays first."

INTERVIEWER: "I'm sorry. We do not discuss salary over the phone."

APPLICANT: "Ohhh . . . I see . . . Does it pay above the minimum wage?"

INTERVIEWER: "Sir, we do not discuss salary over the phone. You will have to come in for an interview."

APPLICANT: "Okay. I just thought . . ."

INTERVIEWER: "When can you come in?"

APPLICANT: "How about Thursday . . . no, no . . . Friday would be better. I have a game Thursday."

INTERVIEWER: (Silence . . .)

APPLICANT: "Must I come at any special time on Friday?"

INTERVIEWER: "No."

1. How do you think the applicant handled this phone interview? Explain.

_____

_____

2. Did he achieve his goal? Why or why not?

_____

_____

Major department store needs sales-clerks w/experience. H.S. grads only. Some college preferred. Call Anne Hutchinson for interview appointment. 555–1890

Applicant's goals:

Joan Pillerman is calling in reference to this job. Joan's qualifications match those outlined. Joan's goal: an interview.

SWITCHBOARD OPERATOR: "Bergman's Department Store."

JOAN: "Anne Hutchinson, please."

SWITCHBOARD OPERATOR: "Is she with personnel?"

JOAN: "Yes, I think so."

SWITCHBOARD OPERATOR: (Rings Personnel)

ANNE HUTCHINSON: "Personnel Department, Miss Hutchinson."

JOAN: "Is this *Anne* Hutchinson?"

ANNE HUTCHINSON: "Yes, it is."

JOAN: "My name is Joan Pillerman. I'm calling about your ad in today's paper. Do you still have openings for salesclerks?"

ANNE HUTCHINSON: "Yes, we do."

JOAN: "I would like to come in for an interview."

ANNE HUTCHINSON: "Are you a high school graduate?"

JOAN: "Yes, and I'm taking evening classes in business management at the Community College."

ANNE HUTCHINSON: "Oh, that's great! How about tomorrow morning at 9:00, Joan?"

JOAN: "Tomorrow morning at nine would be fine."

ANNE HUTCHINSON: "Do you know where Bergman's is located?"

JOAN: "Yes, I do."

ANNE HUTCHINSON: "Come to the personnel office. We're on the eighth floor."

JOAN: "Thank you . I'll see you tomorrow morning at nine."

1. How do you think the applicant handled this phone interview? Explain. _____

_____

_____

2. Did she achieve her goal? Why or why not? _____

_____

_____

Taking telephone messages

After you are on the job, the phone will still be important. Almost everyone has had to leave a telephone message. Have you ever taken a telephone message? Did you tell the person who received the call what the other person said? Did you write a memo? Communicating by phone is a skill you need at home and on the job.

Whether the message you take is personal or job related, there are certain skills you must have. First, you must know *what* information a message should have. How do you decide this? Ask yourself what *you* would want to know if you got a telephone message. What do you expect when someone says, "Anne called"? The person taking the message "Anne called" has already told you who called. You might ask, "What did Anne want?" or "What was the message?" Not everyone leaves a message, especially friends and family. Sometimes people just call. But the person who wasn't in may still have questions. He or she may want to know who called and WHEN they called. Sometimes the person calling may leave a telephone number. This person wants you to know HOW TO REACH them. When you take a phone message, find out:

- Who is calling
- When (the time of the call)
- What is the message
- How to reach the caller

Read the call memo below. It is a job memo. Does it answer *WHO CALLED?* *WHEN? WHAT* was said? *HOW TO REACH THE CALLER?*

CALL MEMO

(IMPORTANT MESSAGE)

FOR _Anne Smith_

DATE _5-16_ TIME _10:15_ **(A.M.)** P.M.

M _Mr. Robert Grimes_

OF _Best Value Office Supply_

PHONE _555-0810_

AREA CODE / NUMBER / EXTENSION

TELEPHONED	✓	PLEASE CALL	
CAME TO SEE YOU		WILL CALL AGAIN	
WANTS TO SEE YOU		RUSH	
RETURNED YOUR CALL		SPECIAL ATTENTION	

MESSAGE _Your order will be ready Thursday._

SIGNED _Janet Walters_

LITHO IN U.S.A.

TOPS ● FORM 3002P

On the job, there are likely to be many telephone calls each day. Some of these people may not leave a message. They may simply call back later. But it's a good idea to ask, "Is there a message?" If the person does not tell you a telephone number, you could ask, "Is there a number where you can be reached?" You have to follow the flow of the conversation. For example, the memo above resulted from this phone conversation.

JANET WALTERS: "Janet Walters, Quick Copy Printing."

ROBERT GRIMES: "This is Best Value Office Supply. Is Anne Smith in?"

JANET WALTERS: "No, Ms. Smith is out of the office at the moment."

ROBERT GRIMES: "Well, just tell her that her order will be ready Thursday."

JANET WALTERS: (writing . . .) "Her order will be ready Thursday."

ROBERT GRIMES: "Yeah, that's right."

JANET WALTERS: "And you're with . . . ?"

ROBERT GRIMES: "Best Value Office Supply. I'm Robert Grimes."

JANET WALTERS: "Is there a number where Ms. Smith can reach you?"

ROBERT GRIMES: "Yes. 555–0010."

Janet Walters had to question the caller. She wanted to leave a complete message for Anne Smith. If Ms. Smith has a question about the order, she can call Robert Grimes at 555–0010. If she doesn't remember the salesman, Robert Grimes, she will find the company's name on the memo. And you will recall that the memo had the message, "Your order will be ready Thursday." Janet Walters took a very effective memo. It answered:

• Who called	Robert Grimes, Best Value Office Supply
• When	10:15, May 16
• The message	"Your order will be ready Thursday."
• How to reach the caller	555–0010

Janet's message was also brief. She only wrote the important details. You should notice that Janet Walters did not say where Ms. Smith was when Robert Grimes called. It would *not* be proper to say "Ms. Smith is not back from lunch yet, " or "Ms. Smith is late for work this morning."

ACTIVITY 13
Taking phone messages

Pretend that you are the receptionist handling the following call. Read the conversation carefully. Then write the information required by the call memo.

Time: 9:40 A.M.

RECEPTIONIST: "This is Baker and Bailey Law Firm. May I help you?"

CLIENT: "This is Robert Whitney. I'd like to speak with Mr. Baker about a case he's handling for me."

RECEPTIONIST: "Mr. Baker is not in."

CLIENT: "When do you expect him?"

RECEPTIONIST: "He'll be in after lunch."

CLIENT: "I'll try again after 2:00. If I don't reach him today, will you have him call me tomorrow at my home? The telephone number is 555–0703. Thank you."

```
┌─────────────────────────────────────────────┐
│        ╭──────────────────────────╮          │
│        │  IMPORTANT MESSAGE       │          │
│        ╰──────────────────────────╯          │
│                                              │
│   FOR _____         │
│                                    A.M.      │
│   DATE _____ TIME _____  P.M.       │
│                                              │
│   M _____         │
│                                              │
│   OF _____         │
│                                              │
│   PHONE _____         │
│         AREA CODE   NUMBER   EXTENSION        │
│   ┌──────────────────┬──────────────────┐    │
│   │ TELEPHONED       │ PLEASE CALL      │    │
│   ├──────────────────┼──────────────────┤    │
│   │ CAME TO SEE YOU  │ WILL CALL AGAIN  │    │
│   ├──────────────────┼──────────────────┤    │
│   │ WANTS TO SEE YOU │ RUSH             │    │
│   ├──────────────────┼──────────────────┤    │
│   │ RETURNED YOUR CALL│ SPECIAL ATTENTION│   │
│   └──────────────────┴──────────────────┘    │
│                                              │
│   MESSAGE _____         │
│   _____          │
│   _____          │
│   _____          │
│   _____          │
│   _____          │
│   _____          │
│                                              │
│   SIGNED _____         │
│   LITHO IN U.S.A.                            │
└─────────────────────────────────────────────┘
```

TOPS ▼ FORM 3002P

- In this conversation, you are Tracy E. Johnson, a co-worker of John Penn. Read the talk that follows. Then write the memo just as Tracy would. Be sure to initial the memo.

3:30 P.M.

TRACY JOHNSON: "John Penn's line . . . Tracy Johnson speaking. May I help you?"

ARNOLD JENKINS: "Yes. This is Arnold Jenkins of Whitney Electronics. I'd like to speak with Mr. Penn if that's possible."

TRACY JOHNSON: (Leaves the phone) "I'm sorry, I'm unable to locate Mr. Penn. May I take a message?"

ARNOLD JENKINS: "Tell him that I will have the information he asked for tomorrow morning at 9 o'clock."

TRACY JOHNSON: "Does Mr. Penn have your number?"

ARNOLD JENKINS: "You'd better take it. He may wish to call me today. It's 252–0401, area code 304, extension 21."

TRACY JOHNSON: "Thank you, Mr. Jenkins. I'll see that Mr. Penn gets your message."

```
┌─────────────────────────────────────────┐
│        (IMPORTANT MESSAGE)               │
│                                          │
│  FOR_____       │
│                              A.M.        │
│  DATE_____TIME_____P.M.      │
│                                          │
│  M_____       │
│                                          │
│  OF_____       │
│                                          │
│  PHONE_____       │
│        AREA CODE    NUMBER    EXTENSION   │
│  ┌──────────────┬──┬─────────────┬──┐    │
│  │ TELEPHONED   │  │ PLEASE CALL │  │    │
│  ├──────────────┼──┼─────────────┼──┤    │
│  │ CAME TO SEE  │  │ WILL CALL   │  │    │
│  │ YOU          │  │ AGAIN       │  │    │
│  ├──────────────┼──┼─────────────┼──┤    │
│  │ WANTS TO SEE │  │ RUSH        │  │    │
│  │ YOU          │  │             │  │    │
│  ├──────────────┼──┼─────────────┼──┤    │
│  │ RETURNED     │  │ SPECIAL     │  │    │
│  │ YOUR CALL    │  │ ATTENTION   │  │    │
│  └──────────────┴──┴─────────────┴──┘    │
│                                          │
│  MESSAGE_____       │
│  _____        │
│  _____        │
│  _____        │
│  _____        │
│  _____        │
│  _____        │
│  _____        │
│                                          │
│  SIGNED_____       │
│  LITHO IN U.S.A.                         │
└─────────────────────────────────────────┘

TOPS  FORM 3002P
```

If no printed message forms are available, be sure that you provide the following information on a piece of paper:

- Date and exact time of the phone call

- Correct name, company, and phone number of the caller

- Message

- Desire regarding the return call

- Your name or initials

To make certain you have written the correct information, repeat the message, including the phone number, to the caller for confirmation.

Rewrite the following message in a brief, businesslike form. The message is for David Jacobson.

Today when the phone rang it was Jim from the bookstore on the corner called Jim Brown's Bookstore. He said that your order has been held up. He said that you ordered a book called *How to Write a Resume.* The book will probably be in on January 1. He will call you when the book comes in. He kept being interrupted by customers, but he said his telephone number is 555–4582.

Fill in the blank spaces in the following statements. Choose words that are appropriate and businesslike.

1. (Your boss has been at lunch for the past two hours. You answer his calls.)

"Mr. Greene is _____ . May I help you?"

2. (You are calling Burger Barn about a part-time job that was advertised in the newspaper.)

"Hello. I _____ about _____ ."

3. (Your boss, Mr. Greene, wants to make an appointment with Ms. Carolyn Benson of Northwest Industries. She is expecting him to call. He asks you to make the call asking for an appointment either Monday or Tuesday morning.)

"Hello. This is _____ . I am calling for _____ . Mr. Greene would like to _____

_____ ."

4. (You are calling Ajax Manufacturing about a part-time warehouse job. You want to know if after-school hours are available.)

"Hello. I _____ about _____ . I need to know _____

_____ ."

5. (You want to get a part-time job. You would like to work at the department store where your friend works. They have not advertised for workers. But you decide to call and inquire.)

"Hello. I would like _____ . Will you please tell me _____ ."

SHOW WHAT YOU KNOW . . .

About Telephone Skills

Select a partner to role-play the telephone situation described below.

PARTNER 1: You are calling about a job as a stock person advertised in the local newspaper. The person you need to speak to is Marci Snead. She is not in at this time. You want to leave her a message and want her to call you back.

PARTNER 2: You are the switchboard operator at Roosevelt Department Store. You receive a call intended for Marci Snead. The person is asking about a job as stock person. You must take the message for Ms. Snead. Be sure to get all of the information she will need to return the call.

Help-wanted ads

Newspapers charge for classified ads. The longer the ad, the more you pay. People buying ad space usually try to write short ads. To read classified ads, you must know what the abbreviations stand for. Job ads, like all classified ads, may have abbreviations and leave out words.

The name of a job is often shortened. An ad may show a typist job as "TYPST." An opening for a manager could appear as "MGR. WANTED." Look at the job ad abbreviations above. How many of them do you know?

Job ads can be found in the classified section of your newspaper. These ads may have the heading "Help Wanted." They may also appear under headings such as "Employment" or "Employment Opportunity." The help-wanted section is a good source for job leads. There are usually a lot of different job openings listed in this section of the paper. These ads tell you the types of jobs that are open. They also tell you how to apply for a particular job. Many ads tell you how much education you need. Some ads tell you if experience is necessary to get a certain job. Some ads give information about pay, hours, and benefits.

Type of job •———————

Experience and/or • education needed

> Bus Boys and Girls—Good for H.S. students; afternoon and evening hours; experience preferred but will train; apply in person. Mable's Restaurant, 567 Main St.

———• Hours to work

———• How to apply

ACTIVITY 14
Reading want ad abbreviations

For this activity, match the want ad abbreviations in column A with the words in column B.

	A		B
———	1. ass't.	**a.**	education
———	2. pref'd.	**b.**	department
———	3. educ.	**c.**	minimum
———	4. min.	**d.**	license
———	5. temp.	**e.**	weekly
———	6. dpt.	**f.**	preferred
———	7. lic.	**g.**	assistant
———	8. trnee.	**h.**	veteran
———	9. vet.	**i.**	trainee
———	10. wkly.	**j.**	temporary

ACTIVITY 15
Reading want ad abbreviations

The help-wanted ads below contain abbreviations. Words are left out, too. In this activity, you are to write out each ad in words. If you see an unfamiliar abbreviation, try to use the words you do know as clues to identify it.

Example:

SEC'Y WANTED.
    F/T
Work with exec.
in office bldg.
in downtown loc.
Type 45 w.p.m.
Call 999-8383 for appt.
M/F

SECRETARY WANTED
    Full Time
Work with executive
in office building
in downtown location.
Type 45 words per minute.
Call 999-8383 for appointment.
Male/Female.

1. Apt. Mgr.
   Exp. for new high-rise
   bldg., salary, apt., and
   incentives.

_____

_____

_____

_____

_____

2. Sec'y.
   Appliance store.
   Answer phone, file, no
   exp. nec., but must type
   60 w.p.m.

   _____

   _____

   _____

   _____

3. Fitters.
   5 yrs. exper. Good wages
   and bfts.

   _____

   _____

   _____

   _____

4. Die Makers
   Day wk. Full bfts.

   _____

   _____

   _____

   _____

5. Quality Control Asst.
   2 yrs. exp. req'd. in
   automotive, gd. wages,
   bfts.

   _____

   _____

   _____

   _____

6. Lab Tech.
   All-around plate man.
   Permanent position,
   excel. conditions &
   salary.

   _____

   _____

   _____

   _____

SHOW WHAT YOU KNOW . . .

About Help-Wanted Ads

Write a help-wanted ad for your "ideal" teacher. Use at least five (5) of the abbreviations given in this section.

ACTIVITY 16
Reading want ads for information

The want ads below are typical job ads. Notice that these ads are set up in alphabetical order. Words are left out of these ads. Only key words and phrases are used. Read each ad carefully. Then complete the statements below.

DISHWASHER—Exper. only need apply. 151 East Street. Call Larry 555-5035.	KITCHEN HELPER Must be dependable. Good bfts. Call at the Money Tree, 222 Lane St. bet. 2:30–5:30 p.m.
EXECUTIVE TRAINEE H.S.G. or some college. No exp. nec. Acme Personnel, 555-1200.	LABORERS—General factory work, hard shoes, report ready to work 5:30 a.m. and 2 p.m. 1947 River Rd.
FASHION MODELS Men 5'8" or taller, Women 5'2" or taller needed for commercials, fashion and product advertising, Ms. Modeling Agency, 555-9683.	PIZZA MAKER Exp. only. Good wages, full or part time. After 2 p.m. 555-7380.

1. The jobs that require previous experience are ———————————————————————— .

2. You may apply for the kitchen helper's job at——————— between the hours of ——————— .

3. The executive trainee job is being handled by ——————————————— .

4. You would call ————————————————————— about the fashion model's job.

5. For the laborer's job you must bring ———————————————— and be ready to work.

ACTIVITY 17
Looking for specific jobs in the want ads

1. Look in the want ad section of your local newspaper for job openings for the following types of workers.
   a. Typist—no experience
   b. Secretary—on one year's experience
   c. Laborer—no experience
   d. Waitperson/Server—some experience
   e. Busser/Busperson—six months' experience

2. How would you apply for these positions? List telephone numbers, addresses, person(s) to contact, and any other useful information.

   Typist ——————————————————————————————————

Secretary _____

_____

Laborer _____

_____

Server _____

_____

Busser _____

_____

ACTIVITY 18
Using the help-wanted section of the newspaper

Have you ever read the help-wanted section of a newspaper for a large city? If you have, you know that there are a variety of jobs advertised. Use these ads from a city paper to answer the questions below.

031 HELP WANTED	031 HELP WANTED
ARCADE ATTENDANT 5–10 p.m. 555-6801	SERVERS—wanted Burger Basement, min. 3 yrs. exper. Apply in person, bet. 7–9 p.m. Mon.–Fri., 33205 Oak, Landview.
BEAUTICIANS—Exp. Prefer clientele—555-1410	STOCK PERSON—No exp. nec. 555-9801 aft. 3
BOOKKEEPER Full charge, exp. 10 hrs. wkly. Westwood area. P.O. Box 8170, Westwood	TYPIST—40 wpm, p.t. 3–6 p.m. 555-7870
CAB DRIVER—Exp'd only. 555-4888 aft. 5	USED CAR BUMP MAN Work on salary, must have tools. Tom or Jim, 555-7272 aft. 10
CAREER MINDED Pay-TV installers. Top wages, need tools. Send resume to Box C–1605, Local Press, Springfield.	WAIT STAFF experienced, good tips, apply in person only. Pine Valley Diner, 16 Elm Street, Pine Valley.
CASHIER COUNTER Help Needed Now—Call today, good pay. Call Job Finders, Inc. $60 fee. 555-8400.	

1. Which number could you call if you were interested in a typist's job? _____

2. How many openings are there for a cab driver? _____

3. If you are a pay-TV installer, where can you send your resume? _____

4. What number would you call if you wanted a job as an arcade attendant? _____

5. Where can a person with no job experience apply? _____

6. Which company charges a fee for locating jobs? _____

46

Write out the full word for each abbreviation.

1. exp. _____

2. ass't. _____

3. pref'd. _____

4. sal. _____

5. sec'y. _____

6. educ. _____

7. p/t _____

8. wkly. _____

9. trnee. _____

10. dpt. _____

Select the phrase that correctly completes each sentence.

_____ **11.** To find the job listings for part-time waitstaff, you must
   a. look through all the job ads.
   b. find the section labeled "Waitstaff" or "Restaurant"
   c. find the sections labeled "Waitstaff" or "Restaurant" and "Part-time."

_____ **12.** When an ad says "min. 3 yrs. exp." and you have six months of experience, you should
   a. make an application anyway.
   b. lie about your experience.
   c. keep looking for a job ad that matches your experience and skills.

_____ **13.** When a job ad says "apply in person" you should
   a. write a letter and drop it off at the address in the ad.
   b. telephone the place.
   c. go directly to the address in the ad yourself.

_____ **14.** When an ad says "must be dependable," the employer will be looking for a person who
   a. arrives regularly and on time.
   b. has a good appearance.
   c. lives nearby.

_____ **15.** Ads for secretaries often say "must type 60 w.p.m." or "must type 40 w.p.m." This probably means
   a. you can simply say that your typing meets their requirements.
   b. you could be given a typing test.
   c. you simply need to be able to do some typing.

Filling out forms

Have you ever applied for a library card? Did you sign up for the school soccer team? Perhaps you have ordered something from a catalog or applied for a social security card. We fill out forms for lots of reasons. They are a necessary part of our lives.

In filling out any form you need to know two things: (1) what you have been asked, and (2) how and where to write the answers. This chapter will teach you the language of forms. You will learn the vocabulary you need in filling out applications. This will help you understand what you have been asked. You will also learn where and how to write your answers.

First you will study some forms you see every day. Examples are an application for a library card and a voter registration form. You will study an application for a social security number. Then you will study and practice writing checks, filling out deposit slips, and keeping a check register. You will learn about consumer credit applications. You will also practice filling out a catalog order form.

Everyday forms

WORDS TO KNOW

applicant's signature   your name written out

apt.   apartment

disability   any physical or medical problem that might affect your ability to drive or work

in lieu of   in place of

maiden name   the last name of an unmarried woman

mailing address   address to which your mail is sent

mandatory   required, such as proof of age

native-born   born in the country (not state) shown on the form

naturalized   not native-born; became a citizen of the country shown on the form

occupation   what you do for a living

restriction   limitation; something you should not or cannot do

revoke   to take back; cancel

suspend   to come to a stop, usually for a short time

valid   proper; legal

voluntary answer   an answer that you may or may not choose to give

witness   person who writes his or her name on a form to show that he or she saw someone else sign it

Study the words in the *Words to Know* section. Knowing these words will help you do the activities in this section.

ACTIVITY 1
Understanding the vocabulary of everyday forms

Match the words in Column A with their definitions in Column B.

A

_____ 1. disability

_____ 2. native-born

_____ 3. mandatory

_____ 4. revoke

_____ 5. in lieu of

_____ 6. restriction

_____ 7. occupation

_____ 8. suspend

_____ 9. witness

_____ 10. valid

B

A. person who signs a form to show he or she saw someone else sign it

B. limitation

C. physical or mental problem that might affect your ability to drive or work

D. in place of

E. proper; legal

F. born in the country shown on the form

G. required

H. what you do for a living

I. to take back; cancel

J. to come to a stop, usually for a short time

Complete the statements below using words from the *Words to Know* list.

11. The examiner asked whether my driver's license had been _____

    or _____ .

12. I can drive to the lake because my driver's license is still _____ .

13. You may be asked whether your driver's license is being held _____ bail.

14. I became a _____ citizen last October.

15. Is it _____ to show a birth certificate to get a social

    security card?

Always briefly look over a form before you fill it out. Determine *how* and *where* to write your responses. For example, a form may require that you print or type your answers. It may require that you write in *ink*. There may be sections that don't apply to you. You may be asked to write your last name first. You may have to write smaller than you usually do.

Most people fill in the information on a form as they come to it. Here are examples of what can happen when you do this:

```
                       ⎯(Maiden name)
                    ↙
Name  Georgiana(Wright)Power   SS#  000·00·000

Address  _____411  Park Avenue_____

         _____East Orange, New Jersey_____

Maiden Name  ____Georgiana Wright_____
```

Georgiana Power wanted the person inspecting this form to know her former name. Notice that she included her maiden name on the first line. If she had skimmed the entire application first, she would have seen the space provided for this information.

```
Name                                    Age   Sex
      Lynda  Coles                      18    F

Address
      118 Woodlawn, Berlaire, Maryland

Home phone              Work phone
     555·7210              555-1304

Occupation
     Short  Order  Cook

Soc. Sec. No.   000-14-1910
              DO NOT WRITE BELOW THIS LINE
```

Lynda Coles ran out of space before answering all of the questions. She still had to give her social security number. All the information requested should have been written *above* the lines, *not below*.

50

Name
Pamela Hughes

Address
1181 Congress Ave., Apt. 8-J, ~~Columbus Ohio 43012~~

City
Columbus

State
Ohio

ZIP Code
43012

SS
000-10-6191

Birth Date
2 10 76
M   D   Yr

Some of the information on this form has been crossed out. Pamela Hughes filled in her complete address on the line requesting address. She later realized that the address line was for the street. A different space was provided for city, state, and ZIP Code.

REGISTRATION FORM

All classes meet at Mountain View Community Center, 55 E. Valley Rd., Mountain View, Colorado. Enrollments are limited and registration is on a first-come, first-served basis. Registration must be accompanied by payment. Classes are $40 each.

Name _____SANCHEZ_____ _____RAFAEL_____
          LAST   FIRST

Address __414 N. PINE__ Apt. __212__

City __MOUNTAIN VIEW__ State __CO__ ZIP _____

I wish to take the following class(es):

_____ Woodworking

_____ Cooking

_____ Spanish

_____ English

_____ Sewing

_____ Accounting

_____ Auto Repair

I enclose the amount of

$ _____

Make checks payable to Mountain View Community Center.

Signature:

_____

DO NOT WRITE ON THIS SIDE

Date received __AUG. 3, 1994__

Payment _____

No. of classes _____

Enrollment _____ WW
            _____ C
            _____ S
            _____ E
            _____ SE
            _____ A

This applicant started to complete his registration without reading over the form. He dropped down to Name and began writing. As he worked *across* the form, he saw Date received. He started to fill out these blanks also. The heading above reads DO NOT WRITE ON THIS SIDE.

Always look over a form before filling it out. Make all answers neat and complete. The information requested may differ from form to form, but there are certain questions you can be ready to answer. Always know who your references are. Know what county you live in. Know your phone number and your social security number. If you are applying for a driver's license, have your driver's education certificate handy. You may be asked about it. If you are applying for a student loan, you may be asked about your income or your parents' income. One day you may be filling out a voter registration form. Know the name of your county or township. An application should always be as *complete* as possible.

ACTIVITY 2
Completing forms

Complete the forms below as neatly and accurately as possible.

PUBLIC LIBRARY

APPLICATION FOR LIBRARY CARD

NAME _____

ADDRESS _____

      City   State ZIP   County

TELEPHONE _____ BIRTH DATE _____
                                   M D YR

    I understand that I must abide by all rules and regulations of this library and all city branches.

          Signature _____

For your free Kentucky travel packet, call toll-free or write:
Travel, Dept. ML-02, Box 2011, Frankfort, KY 40602.

Name _____

Address _____

City _____ State _____ Zip _____

The Uncommon Wealth of
KENTUCKY
1-800-225-TRIP

ACTIVITY 3 Study the next form and answer the questions.

Voter registration forms

VOTER REGISTRATION FORM
PLEASE PRINT IN INK OR TYPE

1 Name of the registrant (Please Print):
Patterson,   *Lance*   *Adam*
LAST   FIRST   MIDDLE

2 Residence of the registrant:
803 Long Lake Road | APARTMENT NUMBER
STREET ADDRESS
Elizabeth   *Union*   *07201*
MUNICIPALITY   COUNTY   ZIP

3 Rural Mailing Address (if any):

R.D. NUMBER   BOX   MUNICIPALITY   ZIP

4 This form is being used as (Check One):
☑ New Registration ☐ Change of Address ☐ Change of Name

5 Birth Date:
12 | *19* | *74*
MONTH   DAY   YEAR

6 From what address did you last register to vote, and under what name?

LAST NAME   FIRST   MIDDLE

STREET ADDRESS   APARTMENT NUMBER

MUNICIPALITY   COUNTY   STATE   ZIP

7 I am a ☑ native born ☐ naturalized citizen (Check One).
I was naturalized:

MONTH   DAY   YEAR   MUNICIPALITY   STATE

8 By the time of the next general election, I will be at least 18 years of age, I will be a citizen of the United States, and I will have resided in this State at least 30 days and in the county of ___*Union*___ at least 30 days. To the best of my knowledge and belief, all the foregoing statements made by me are true and correct. I understand that any false or fraudulent registration or attempted registration may subject me to a fine of up to $1,000.00 or imprisonment of up to 5 years, or both pursuant to R.S. 19:34-1.

Lance A. Patterson | *10-21-93*
SIGNATURE OR MARK OF THE REGISTRANT   DATE OF SIGNATURE

9 I, being a registered voter in ___*Union*___ county in the State of New Jersey, witnessed the making of the above signature or mark.
Vaughn P. Jonas | *10-21-93*
SIGNATURE OF THE WITNESS   DATE OF WITNESSING
Vaughn P. Jonas
NAME OF THE WITNESS (Please Print):
816 Long Lake Road, Elizabeth   *Union*   *07201*
STREET ADDRESS OF THE WITNESS   MUNICIPALITY   COUNTY   ZIP

1. The registrant is _____ .

2. He is registering to _____ .

3. He lives at _____ in _____ County.

4. This form is being used as _____ .

5. His witness is _____ .

Application for driver's license

In many states you do not have to fill out an application for a driver's license. Instead, you are asked questions by an employee of a driver's license facility or office. Your answers will then be typed directly into a computer. Your local facility will tell you what you are required to have when you apply for a license. You will probably need identification that will verify your name, your birth date, and your social security number. You may be asked questions like the following. Study these questions as if you were preparing to apply for a license; answer them for yourself.

1. Is your driver's license or privilege to obtain a license suspended, revoked, canceled, or refused in any state under this or any other name? ⸺⸺⸺⸺⸺

2. Do you presently hold a valid driver's license in this or any other state? ⸺⸺⸺⸺

3. Is your driver's license being held in court in lieu of bail? ⸺⸺⸺⸺

4. Do you have any condition that might cause a temporary loss of consciousness? (If yes, a physician's statement is required.) ⸺⸺⸺⸺

5. Do you have any mental or physical condition that might interfere with safe driving?

⸺⸺⸺⸺⸺⸺⸺⸺

Application for a social security card

One of the most important forms you will ever complete is your application for a social security number. Everyone in the United States who has a job should have a social security card. Your social security card shows your social security number. Tax laws require that taxpayers show social security numbers for their dependents on tax forms. Children now receive social security numbers before they enter school. Should you ever apply for social security benefits, you will need your social security number.

If you were born in the United States and have never had a social security number, you must show documents that give your age and citizenship. You will need to show your birth certificate and some form of identification.

If you are a U.S. citizen who was born outside the United States, you will need your consular report of birth, if you have one. You will also need one form of identification. If you do not have your consular report of birth, you will need your foreign birth certificate and one of the following: a U.S. Citizen ID card, U.S. passport, Certificate of Citizenship, or a Certificate of Naturalization.

Here are some examples of the kinds of documents that will show who you are.

- Driver's license

- U.S. government or state employee ID card

- Passport

- School ID card, record, or report card

- Marriage or divorce record

- Health insurance card

- Clinic, doctor, or hospital records

- Military records

- Court order for name change

- Adoption records

- Church membership or confirmation record (if not used as evidence of age)

- Insurance policy

- Any other document that establishes your identity

ACTIVITY 4
Filling out an application for a social security card

Study the social security card application on the next page including the instructions at the top. Decide whether the statements below are TRUE (T) or FALSE (F).

——— 1. You may print on the application form.

——— 2. You may use a typewriter to complete the form.

——— 3. You may complete the form in red ink.

——— 4. You may skip question 5—Race/Ethnic Description.

——— 5. If you give false information on the form, you may be sent to prison.

SOCIAL SECURITY ADMINISTRATION
Application for a Social Security Card

Form Approved
OMB No. 0960-0066

INSTRUCTIONS

- Please read "How To Complete This Form" on page 2.
- Print or type using black or blue ink. DO NOT USE PENCIL.
- After you complete this form, take or mail it along with the required documents to your nearest Social Security office.
- If you are completing this form for someone else, answer the questions as they apply to that person. Then, sign your name in question 16.

1 NAME
To Be Shown On Card

▶ FIRST _____ FULL MIDDLE NAME _____ LAST

FULL NAME AT BIRTH IF OTHER THAN ABOVE

FIRST _____ FULL MIDDLE NAME _____ LAST

OTHER NAMES USED _____

2 MAILING ADDRESS
Do Not Abbreviate

▶ STREET ADDRESS, APT. NO., PO BOX, RURAL ROUTE NO.

CITY _____ STATE _____ ZIP CODE

3 CITIZENSHIP
(Check One)

☐ U.S. Citizen ☐ Legal Alien Allowed To Work ☐ Legal Alien Not Allowed To Work ☐ Foreign Student Allowed Restricted Employment ☐ Conditionally Legalized Alien Allowed To Work ☐ Other (See Instructions On Page 2)

4 SEX

☐ Male ☐ Female

5 RACE/ETHNIC DESCRIPTION
(Check One Only—Voluntary)

☐ Asian, Asian-American Or Pacific Islander ☐ Hispanic ☐ Black (Not Hispanic) ☐ North American Indian Or Alaskan Native ☐ White (Not Hispanic)

6 DATE OF BIRTH
MONTH DAY YEAR

7 PLACE OF BIRTH
(Do Not Abbreviate) CITY _____ STATE OR FOREIGN COUNTRY _____ FCI

☐ Office Use Only

8 MOTHER'S MAIDEN NAME

FIRST _____ FULL MIDDLE NAME _____ LAST NAME AT HER BIRTH

9 FATHER'S NAME

FIRST _____ FULL MIDDLE NAME _____ LAST

10 Has the person in item 1 ever applied for or received a Social Security number before?

☐ Yes (If "yes", answer questions 11-13.) ☐ No (If "no", go on to question 14.) ☐ Don't Know (If "don't know", go on to question 14.)

11 Enter the Social Security number previously assigned to the person listed in item 1.

☐☐☐ – ☐☐ – ☐☐☐☐

12 Enter the name shown on the most recent Social Security card issued for the person listed in item 1.

FIRST _____ MIDDLE _____ LAST

13 Enter any different date of birth if used on an earlier application for a card.

MONTH _____ DAY _____ YEAR

14 TODAY'S DATE ▶ MONTH DAY YEAR   **15 DAYTIME PHONE NUMBER** ▶ ( ) AREA CODE

DELIBERATELY FURNISHING (OR CAUSING TO BE FURNISHED) FALSE INFORMATION ON THIS APPLICATION IS A CRIME PUNISHABLE BY FINE OR IMPRISONMENT, OR BOTH.

16 YOUR SIGNATURE

▶ _____

17 YOUR RELATIONSHIP TO THE PERSON IN ITEM 1 IS:

☐ Self ☐ Natural Or Adoptive Parent ☐ Legal Guardian ☐ Other (Specify) _____

DO NOT WRITE BELOW THIS LINE (FOR SSA USE ONLY)

NPN		DOC	NTI	CAN		ITV
PBC	EVI	EVA	EVC	NWR	DNR	UNIT

EVIDENCE SUBMITTED

SIGNATURE AND TITLE OF EMPLOYEE(S) REVIEWING EVIDENCE AND/OR CONDUCTING INTERVIEW

DATE

DCL   DATE

Form **SS-5** (5/88)   1/85, 8/85, and 11/86 editions may be used until supply is exhausted

Look at the blank social security application form on page 56. Fill out the application as if *you* are applying for a social security number.

SHOW WHAT YOU KNOW . . .

About Forms

Assume that you are in charge of a summer art and craft show in your community. Design an entry form for those who want to display their work.

Bank forms

Banks offer their customers many money-related services. They loan money for buying cars. They sell savings bonds. They make loans for home improvements. They also provide checking accounts so people need not carry large sums of cash. People put money into a checking account. Then they write checks on the money they have deposited. They use checks just as other people use money. They pay bills. They buy things. They pay the rent. The bank gives each checking customer an account number. Each customer has personalized checks in a checkbook. Personalized checks have the customer's name and address on them. These checks have printed numbers.

Study the sample. It shows you how to fill out a check.

Date •

Name of • person or business being paid

Dollar • amount in words; cents as a fraction

JAMES C. OR MARY A. MORRISON
1765 SHERIDAN DRIVE
YOUR CITY, STATE   12345

126

① Jan. 6   19 94   00-6789/0000

② PAY TO THE ORDER OF   Joey's Cleaners & Laundry $8.23   ③

④ Eight and 23/100   DOLLARS

THE BANK OF YOUR CITY
YOUR CITY, USA 12345

MEMO

⑤ Mary Morrison   SAMPLE VOID

⑈000067894⑈ ⑈23456781⑈

Signature of account holder •   Amount in figures •

Checks   This check was written by Mary A. Morrison. She and her husband, James C. Morrison, have a joint checking account with a bank in the town where they live. Their account number is on the check. It's 12345678. On January 6, 1994, Mary wrote check number 126 to Joey's Cleaners & Laundry. The check was for $8.23. Here are the steps Mary took to write this check:

① She filled in the *date* she wrote the check.

② She wrote the name of the business receiving the check. *Pay to the order of* refers to the name of the person, organization, or business you are paying.

③ She wrote the *amount* of the check in figures.

④ The dollar amount was then written in words. The 23¢ was shown as a fraction of a dollar, or 23/100.

$8.23 =   Eight and 23/100   DOLLARS
or
Eight and   23/100   DOLLARS

Mary filled in the entire *dollars line.* Notice that the word *and* divides the dollar amount from the cents. The wavy line fills the entire space. This keeps others from changing the amount of the check.

⑤ Mary wrote her *signature* last. This check is good only if Mary or her husband signs it.

Did you notice the memo space on this check? Some people like to note the purpose of a check here.

ACTIVITY 5
Filling in the "dollars" line

Write the following amounts as they should appear on the dollars line. You may use either method. Remember to use "and" to divide the dollars from the cents.

Example:

$7.29 *Seven and 29/100* _____ DOLLARS

1. $5.26 _____ DOLLARS

2. $23.01 _____ DOLLARS

3. $15.29 _____ DOLLARS

4. $121.00 _____ DOLLARS

5. $51.82 _____ DOLLARS

6. $342.21 _____ DOLLARS

7. $85.50 _____ DOLLARS

8. $92.28 _____ DOLLARS

9. $247.18 _____ DOLLARS

10. $92.28 _____ DOLLARS

ACTIVITY 6
Writing checks

Pretend you are Mary A. Morrison or James C. Morrison. You have a checking account with a bank where you live. Write a check for each of the following situations. Use today's date.

1. You owe Payne's Department Store a payment of $10.30. Today you write them check #127.

JAMES C. OR MARY A. MORRISON 1765 SHERIDAN DRIVE YOUR CITY, STATE 12345	127 _____ 19 ___ 00-6789/0000

PAY TO THE
ORDER OF _____ $

_____ DOLLARS

THE BANK OF YOUR CITY
YOUR CITY, USA 12345

MEMO _____   _____ SAMPLE VOID

⑆000067894⑆ ⑈12345678⑊

2. Next, you write check #128 for $9.17. This check is for Leeds' Variety Store. It is for art supplies. This year you will keep a record of all art expenses. You will list these expenses when you file your tax return at the end of the year. Make a note to yourself in the memo space.

```
                                                          128
      JAMES C. OR MARY A. MORRISON
           1765 SHERIDAN DRIVE
           YOUR CITY, STATE  12345            19        00-6789/0000

   PAY TO THE                                   $
   ORDER OF
                                                          DOLLARS


       THE BANK OF YOUR CITY
       YOUR CITY, USA 12345

   MEMO
                                                   SAMPLE VOID
   ⑆000067894⑆  123456 78⑈
```

3. Write check #129 to the Appalachian Power Company. It's for this month's electric bill. Your account number is 853–470. You owe $29.

```
                                                          129
      JAMES C. OR MARY A. MORRISON
           1765 SHERIDAN DRIVE
           YOUR CITY, STATE  12345            19        00-6789/0000

   PAY TO THE                                   $
   ORDER OF
                                                          DOLLARS


       THE BANK OF YOUR CITY
       YOUR CITY, USA 12345

   MEMO
                                                   SAMPLE VOID
   ⑆000067894⑆  123456 78⑈
```

Deposit slips Before you write checks, you have to put money into your checking account. Your bank will issue you deposit slips. Like your checks, they will most likely have your name printed on them. You will have to fill out a deposit slip when you put money into your checking account.

CHECKING ACCOUNT DEPOSIT TICKET

Cash amount

Account holder's name

JAMES C. OR MARY A. MORRISON
1765 SHERIDAN DRIVE
YOUR CITY, STATE 12345

DATE _Sept. 15_ 19 94

CHECKS AND OTHER ITEMS ARE RECEIVED FOR DEPOSIT
SUBJECT TO THE PROVISIONS OF THE UNIFORM COMMERCIAL
CODE OR ANY APPLICABLE COLLECTION AGREEMENT

DEPOSITED IN

THE BANK OF YOUR CITY
YOUR CITY, USA 12345

⑆000067894⑆ 12345678⑈

Checking account number

CASH →	10	00
LIST CHECKS SINGLY	101	38
	10	00
		00-6789/0000
TOTAL FROM OTHER SIDE		USE OTHER SIDE FOR ADDITIONAL LISTING. ◀ ENTER TOTAL HERE
TOTAL ITEMS TOTAL	121	38

BE SURE EACH ITEM IS PROPERLY ENDORSED

Total deposit

Amount of checks being deposited

ACTIVITY 7
Filling out a deposit slip

Answer these questions about the deposit slip you have just studied.

1. How much cash did James and Mary Morrison deposit? _____

2. What was the date of their deposit? _____

3. Do they have to sign the deposit slip? _____

4. How many checks did they deposit? _____ What was the amount of each check? _____

5. What is the account number? _____

The checkbook register

There are many reasons people use checks instead of cash. For one thing, checks are safe to mail; you can pay bills and buy things without worrying. There is no chance that your money will be lost or stolen. Checks are good records, too. Many banks return the checks paid out of your account with your monthly statement. Your canceled checks become your receipts.

Sometimes, a bank will not pay your check because you don't have enough money in your account. The check is marked "insufficient funds" and is returned to the person or company to whom you wrote it. If your account is overdrawn, you'll be charged an overdraft or penalty fee. The bank notifies you by mail of the overdraft and the resulting charges.

How do you avoid this problem? It is very simple. Use the register that you receive with your checks. Record every check you write in the register. Also list the deposits you make. Some banks charge for each check that you write. Other banks have a monthly service charge. Be sure to record all fees and service charges in your register. Always know how much money you have in your checking account.

Study the sample below. It shows the *single-line* method of entering checks in a register.

RECORD ALL CHARGES OR CREDITS THAT AFFECT YOUR ACCOUNT

NUMBER	DATE	DESCRIPTION OF TRANSACTION	PAYMENT/DEBIT (-)	√ T	FEE (IF ANY) (-)	DEPOSIT/CREDIT (+)	BALANCE	
							$ 1687	42
201	3/7	National Gas Company	$ 55 87		$ 3/7	$ 625 00		
202		Lance Mortgage Co.	250 00					
203		General Telephone Co.	35 68					
204	3/10	Bob's Meat Store	26 89		3/10	300 00	2243	98
205		Leed's Dept. Store	278 19					
206		Cash	200 00					
207		Gus's Service Station	32 41					
208	3/11	Acme Furniture Store	389 88		3/11	200 00	1543	50
209		Easy Credit Card	56 90					
210		Lancaster Hardware	14 26					

REMEMBER TO RECORD AUTOMATIC PAYMENTS / DEPOSITS ON DATE AUTHORIZED.

Occasional balance ●

This checking customer uses each line of the register. All checks and deposits are recorded. A balance is noted from time to time.

The next sample shows the *double-line* method.

Double-Line
Method

Use of two ●
lines for
one entry.
Purpose
of each
check
is stated.

RECORD ALL CHARGES OR CREDITS THAT AFFECT YOUR ACCOUNT

NUMBER	DATE	DESCRIPTION OF TRANSACTION	PAYMENT/DEBIT (-)	√ T	FEE (IF ANY) (-)	DEPOSIT/CREDIT (+)	BALANCE	
							$ 1687	42
201	3/7	National Gas Company	$ 55 87		$	$	55	87
		February Payment					1631	55
202		Lance Mortgage Co.	250 00				250	00
		February House Note					1381	55
203		General Telephone Co.	35 68				35	68
		February Bill					1345	87
		Cash Deposit				625 00	625	00
							1970	87
204		Bob's Meat Store	26 89				26	89
		Steaks					1943	98

REMEMBER TO RECORD AUTOMATIC PAYMENTS / DEPOSITS ON DATE AUTHORIZED.

Balance after each check written ●

In the double-line method, two lines are used for each check written. One line gives the name of the person or business who will get the check. The next line tells what the check is for. The amount of each check is subtracted from the balance. A new balance is shown after each check.

ACTIVITY 8

Keeping a checkbook register

Anne Marie Ramos has a checking account. Below is a page from her register. Study her register. Then answer the questions.

CHECK NO.	DATE	CHECK ISSUED TO	AMOUNT OF CHECK	√	DATE OF DEP.	AMOUNT OF DEPOSIT	BALANCE	
		BALANCE BROUGHT FORWARD →					500	00
863	7/16	Montgomery Ward	10	00				10	00
		Scarf					490	00
864	7/16	Dr. Altchek	50	00				50	00
		Office Visit					440	00
865	7/21	Prudential Insurance	52	50				52	50
		August Premium					381	50
		Cash Deposit			7/22	50	00	50	00
								431	50
866	7/22	Peter Simpson	7	50				7	50
		Gift					430	00
867	7/22	John's Garage	60	00				60	00
		Oil Change					370	00
868	7/23	Montgomery Ward	100	00				100	00
		Drapes					270	00
		Cash Deposit			8/14	100	00	100	00
								370	00

1. What was Anne Marie's balance when she started making entries on this page? _____

2. To whom did she write check #863? _____

3. When did she write this check? _____

4. What did she buy? _____

5. What was the balance after check #864 was written? _____

6. Who received the check? _____

7. What was the balance after check #865 was written? _____

8. What was the last date a deposit was made? _____

9. What was Anne Marie's balance after the deposit was made? _____

10. What was the number of the last check that was written? _____

ACTIVITY 9

Keeping a checkbook register

Record the following items in a checkbook register. Use the *single-line method* and today's date. Begin with check #201.

Checks

Myrtle's Daycare	$35.00
Lum's Drugs	$15.82
Jackson's Dept. Store	$21.00
Consumer's Power	$46.82
Carson's Boutique	$56.94
Ned's Place	$48.52

Deposits

$400.00 (Cash)

RECORD ALL CHARGES OR CREDITS THAT AFFECT YOUR ACCOUNT

NUMBER	DATE	DESCRIPTION OF TRANSACTION	PAYMENT/DEBIT (-)	√T	FEE (IFANY) (-)	DEPOSIT/CREDIT (+)	BALANCE $ 300 00
201			$		$	$	

REMEMBER TO RECORD AUTOMATIC PAYMENTS / DEPOSITS ON DATE AUTHORIZED.

Checking account statements

Each month your bank will mail you a statement of account. This statement shows your checks that came into the bank during the month. It also shows the deposits you made. If there are any other charges, they appear on the statement. Following is a sample of a monthly statement.

Community Trust Bank

STATEMENT OF CHECKING ACCOUNT

PREVIOUS BALANCE $500.00

Account Number 10-437-112

From July 15   to   Aug 14

CHECKS AND CHARGES	DEPOSITS	DATE	BALANCE
10.00		7-18	490.00
50.00		7-18	440.00
	50.00	7-22	490.00
52.50		7-23	437.50
7.50		7-25	430.00
60.00		7-25	370.00

IF   Insufficient Funds
DM   Debit Memo
CM   Credit Memo
SC   Service Charge

BALANCE $370.00

PERIOD ENDING   Aug 14

ACTIVITY 10
Reading a monthly statement

Complete these sentences using the monthly statement above.

1. A monthly statement shows the _____ you wrote and the deposits you made.

2. The statement above begins _____ and goes through _____ .

3. The balance on July 15th was $_____ .

4. The balance at the close of the statement is $ _____ .

5. Five _____ came into the bank during this period.

6. Only one _____ was made.

7. It was for $ _____ .

8. It was made on July _____ .

It is important to compare the bank's records with your records. On page 64 you looked at the checkbook register of Anne Marie Ramos. Then you looked at the statement from Community Trust Bank. Compare these two records. The records do not match exactly. Which check and which deposit do not show on the bank statement?

CHECK YOUR UNDERSTANDING OF BANK FORMS

Write out the following dollar amounts in words. Remember to show cents as a fraction of a dollar.

1. $3.49 _____

2. $43.52 _____

3. $207.09 _____

4. $764.50 _____

5. $25.02 _____

Choose the best answer for the following statements. Write the letter of the answer in the blank.

_____ **6.** A canceled check is a check
    a. with your name printed on it.
    b. the bank has paid and returned to you.
    c. that is no good.

_____ **7.** When a check is endorsed, it
    a. has been received by the writer.
    b. cannot be paid until 30 days after it is written.
    c. has been signed by the person or business to whom it is written.

_____ **8.** A check returned because of "insufficient funds" means
    a. there is not enough money in the account to pay the check.
    b. the bank is in financial trouble and cannot pay the check.
    c. the bank's records are not up to date.

_____ **9.** A check register is a list of
    a. canceled checks.
    b. the checks you have written.
    c. the checks that have been written to you.

_____ **10.** A joint account is an account that
    a. can be used by more than one person.
    b. is good at two different banks.
    c. is good in several states.

Consumer credit applications

When you buy on credit, you buy now and pay later. To get credit you usually have to fill out a credit application. Some people use credit cards. When a credit card is approved, you can buy things and charge them with your card. Sometimes you may make a single, large purchase. It might be for a new car. For some purchases you may need a loan. For large purchases, you will have to fill out a loan application. The money you borrow is paid back in monthly payments that include interest. Before you can get a loan, your credit must be approved.

Credit cards

Look at the following sample credit card application. Most credit applications ask for information about your *work experience, income,* and *credit history.* The company giving credit wants to know (1) if you have a job, (2) how long you've had the job, (3) how much you earn, (4) who you owe, and (5) how promptly you pay.

What you write on the credit card application will help determine if you are a *good credit risk.* Once you sign a credit application, you give permission to have your credit record checked. Your signature also gives the creditor the right to check other information on the application. Most often your *credit references, employment,* and *income* are checked.

You may not get credit if your application is not filled in properly. You probably won't get a chance to explain your answers. Computers are often a part of the processing so you must do it correctly from the start. Study the blank application on the next page carefully.

JCPenney **Credit Application**

Associate Number | 1438 | Account Number

CREDIT INSURANCE ENROLLMENT

Your signature if you wish to insure your credit purchases

YES I wish to protect my JCPenney Account with Credit Insurance for the cost as described above. I understand the insurance is not required.

NO I waive my right to enroll for Credit Insurance at this time.

APPLICANT (SIGN TO ENROLL) | Date of Birth

SPOUSE'S NAME | Date of Birth

In signing this enrollment form, I authorize J.C. Penney Company, Inc. to advance to J.C. Penney Life Insurance Company and J.C. Penney Casualty Insurance Company amounts equal to the premiums becoming due under the policy applied for and bill such amounts with my JCPenney Credit Account. I agree to pay such amounts when billed.

Name of your husband or wife

INFORMATION ABOUT APPLICANT   **PLEASE PRINT**   **An Applicant, if married, may apply for a separate account.**

Your name printed

Your Name (First, Middle Initial, Last) | Social Security Number

Present Street Address | City | State | Zip

Include area code

Home Phone | Business Phone | No. of Dependent Children | None | One | Two | Three | Four or More

How much you pay monthly for where you live

Applicant's Date of Birth | Do You | Own | Rent | Own Mobile Home | Live With Parents | Other (Please Specify) | Monthly Mortgage/ Rent

How Long at This Address | 0 - 6 mos. | 7 mos. - 1 yr. 6 mos. | 1 yr. 7 mos. - 2 yrs. 6 mos. | 2 yrs. 7 mos. - 5 yrs. 6 mos. | 5 yrs. 7 mos. - 8 yrs. 6 mos. | 8 yrs. 7 mos. - 15 yrs. 6 mos. | 15 yrs. 7 mos. or More

Where you lived before you moved to your present address

Former Street Address (If at Current Address Less Than Two Years) | City | State | Zip

Employer's Full Name | Employer's Address (Street, City, State)

How Long on Job | 0 - 6 mos. | 7 mos. - 1 yr. | 1 yr. 1 mo. - 2 yrs. | 2 yrs. 1 mo. - 4 yrs. 6 mos. | 4 yrs. 7 mos. - 6 yrs. 6 mos. | 6 yrs. 7 mos. - 10 yrs. 6 mos. | 10 yrs. 7 mos. or More

Your job title

Present Position | Monthly Salary | Source(s) of Other Income* | Monthly Amount

What you make before deductions

INFORMATION ABOUT (check one) | **Co-Applicant - Also Responsible for Account** | **Authorized Buyer - Allows Other Person to Purchase on Your Account**

Name of person who will share account if you are requesting joint account or name of another person who will use your credit card

Name of Co-Applicant/Authorized Buyer | Relationship to Applicant | Spouse | Other | Social Security Number

This area for information on co-applicant or authorized buyer only

Date of Birth | Business Phone | Employer's Full Name | Employer's Address (Street, City, State)

How Long on Job | 0 - 6 mos. | 7 mos. - 1 yr. | 1 yr. 1 mo. - 2 yrs. | 2 yrs. 1 mo. - 4 yrs. 6 mos. | 4 yrs. 7 mos. - 6 yrs. 6 mos. | 6 yrs. 7 mos. - 10 yrs. 6 mos. | 10 yrs. 7 mos. or More

Present Position | Monthly Salary | Source(s) of Other Income* | Monthly Amount

INFORMATION ABOUT YOUR CREDIT AND OTHER REFERENCES (Include Co-Applicant's, If Joint Account Requested)

Places where you owe or have owed money, such as banks, stores, and credit unions

Bank–Branch | Account in the Name of | Account Number | Checking and Savings/NOW Acct. | Checking | Savings/CD | Loan

Credit Cards: | MasterCard/Visa | AMEX/Diners | Department Store | Other Credit References (List Below)

List Other Credit References (Include Loan or Finance Company) | Firm Name | Location | Account/Loan Number | Account/Loan in the Name of

1.

2.

Name of Nearest Relative Not Living at Address of Applicant or Co-Applicant | Relationship to Applicant | Present Address (Street, City, State) | Home Phone

Sign here to complete your JCPenney Credit Application.
Your Signature(s) mean(s) that you have read, understood, and agree to the terms of the above Retail Installment Credit Agreement.

Applicant Signature | Date | Co-Applicant Signature | B4

*You Need Not Furnish Alimony, Child Support or Separate Maintenance Income Information If You Do Not Want Us to Consider It in Evaluating Your Application.

JCP-2201 (Rev. 11/91) Printed 11/91

AFTER COMPLETING APPLICATION, DETACH AT TOP PERFORATION, FOLD TOP DOWN TO ARROWS, MOISTEN BOTTOM FLAP, FOLD FLAP OVER AND SEAL. POSTAGE PAID BY JCPenney

Study the following credit card application. Answer the questions on page 71.

JCPenney Credit Application

Associate Number	1438	Account Number

CREDIT INSURANCE ENROLLMENT

		APPLICANT (SIGN TO ENROLL)	Date of Birth
☐	**YES** I wish to protect my JCPenney Account with Credit Insurance for the cost as described above. I understand the insurance is not required.		
☒	**NO** I waive my right to enroll for Credit Insurance at this time.	SPOUSE'S NAME	Date of Birth

In signing this enrollment form, I authorize J.C. Penney Company, Inc. to advance to J.C. Penney Life Insurance Company and J.C. Penney Casualty Insurance Company amounts equal to the premiums becoming due under the policy applied for and bill such amounts with my JCPenney Credit Account. I agree to pay such amounts when billed.

INFORMATION ABOUT APPLICANT   **PLEASE PRINT**   An Applicant, if married, may apply for a separate account.

Your Name (First, Middle Initial, Last): **CHARLES E WRIGHT**
Social Security Number: **000726352**

Present Street Address: **5001 Congress Ave. Apt. 3**
City: **Havre DeGrace** State: **MD** Zip: **21078**

Home Phone: **(301) 555-7082** Business Phone: **301 555-7623**
No. of Dependent Children: ☐ None ☐ One ☐ Two ☐ Three ☐ Four or More

Applicant's Date of Birth: **101670**
Do You: ☐ Own ☒ Rent ☐ Own Mobile Home ☐ Live With Parents ☐ Other (Please Specify)
Monthly Mortgage/Rent: **$500**

How Long at This Address: ☐ 0 - 6 mos. ☐ 7 mos. - 1 yr. 6 mos. ☐ 1 yr. 7 mos. - 2 yrs. 6 mos. ☐ 2 yrs. 7 mos. - 5 yrs. 6 mos. ☐ 5 yrs. 7 mos. - 8 yrs. 6 mos. ☐ 8 yrs. 7 mos. - 15 yrs. 6 mos. ☐ 15 yrs. 7 mos. or More

Former Street Address (If at Current Address Less Than Two Years): City: State: Zip:

Employer's Full Name: **Harford Company**
Employer's Address (Street, City, State): **2401 Harvey Aberdeen, Md.**

How Long on Job: ☐ 0 - 6 mos. ☐ 7 mos. - 1 yr. ☐ 1 yr. 1 mo. - 2 yrs. ☒ 2 yrs. 1 mo. - 4 yrs. 6 mos. ☐ 4 yrs. 7 mos. - 6 yrs. 6 mos. ☐ 6 yrs. 7 mos. - 10 yrs. 6 mos. ☐ 10 yrs. 7 mos. or More

Present Position: **Office Manager**
Monthly Salary: **$2500**
Source(s) of Other Income*: Monthly Amount:

INFORMATION ABOUT (check one) ☒ Co-Applicant - Also Responsible for Account   ☐ Authorized Buyer - Allows Other Person to Purchase on Your Account

Name of Co-Applicant/Authorized Buyer: **PATRICIA WRIGHT**
Relationship to Applicant: ☒ Spouse ☐ Other
Social Security Number: **000826977**

Date of Birth: **060470** Business Phone: **301555 8020**
Employer's Full Name: **Harford County Schools**
Employer's Address (Street, City, State): **Bd. of Education Bel Air, MD**

How Long on Job: ☐ 0 - 6 mos. ☒ 7 mos. - 1 yr. ☐ 1 yr. 1 mo. - 2 yrs. ☐ 2 yrs. 1 mo. - 4 yrs. 6 mos. ☐ 4 yrs. 7 mos. - 6 yrs. 6 mos. ☐ 6 yrs. 7 mos. - 10 yrs. 6 mos. ☐ 10 yrs. 7 mos. or More

Present Position: **Teacher**
Monthly Salary: **$2000**
Source(s) of Other Income*: Monthly Amount:

INFORMATION ABOUT YOUR CREDIT AND OTHER REFERENCES (Include Co-Applicant's, If Joint Account Requested)

Bank–Branch: **Raleigh Co. Bank** Account in the Name of: **Charles Wright** Account Number: **7-9-2438-05**
☒ Checking and Savings/NOW Acct. ☒ Checking ☒ Savings/CD ☐ Loan

Credit Cards: ☒ MasterCard/Visa ☐ AMEX/Diners ☒ Department Store ☐ Other Credit References (List Below)

List Other Credit References (Include Loan or Finance Company)

	Firm Name	Location	Account/Loan Number	Account/Loan in the Name of
1.	SMITH'S CLOTHING	Havre DeGrace	64-120-378	CHARLES WRIGHT
2.	SCHOOL EMPLOYEES CREDIT UNION	Bel Air	79-320-900	Patricia Wright

Name of Nearest Relative Not Living at Address of Applicant or Co-Applicant: **FRANCES WRIGHT**
Relationship to Applicant: **Mother**
Present Address (Street, City, State): **122 Grant St., Beckley, WV 25801**
Home Phone: **304 555 5082**

Sign here to complete your JCPenney Credit Application.
Your Signature(s) mean(s) that you have read, understood, and agree to the terms of the above Retail Installment Credit Agreement.

Applicant Signature: **Charles E. Wright** Date: **12-2-94**
Co-Applicant Signature: **Patricia Wright**
B4 ●

*You Need Not Furnish Alimony, Child Support or Separate Maintenance Income Information If You Do Not Want Us to Consider It in Evaluating Your Application.

JCP-2201 (Rev. 11/91) Printed 11/91

↑ ↑ **AFTER COMPLETING APPLICATION, DETACH AT TOP PERFORATION, FOLD TOP DOWN TO ARROWS, MOISTEN BOTTOM FLAP, FOLD FLAP OVER AND SEAL. POSTAGE PAID BY JCPenney**

1. Who is applying for a credit card? ————————————————————

2. How many persons will use this credit account? ————————————

3. Has the applicant lived at 5001 Congress Avenue over one year? ————————

4. Is the applicant buying a home or renting an apartment? ——————————

5. Is the applicant employed? If so, where? ————————————————

6. How much does the applicant earn each month? ——————————————

7. How much does the applicant's spouse earn? ———————————————

8. Does the applicant have a checking account? savings account? bank loan? ————————

9. Who is the applicant's nearest relative not living at his address? ——————————

10. What store does the applicant list as a credit reference? ——————————

——

11. Who is Patricia Wright? ————————————————————————

12. What is her occupation? ————————————————————————

13. Did both applicants sign the application? ————————————————

14. Do you think this applicant will get a credit card? Why or why not? ——————————

ACTIVITY 12
Completing credit card applications

Following is a Montgomery Ward credit application form. Pretend it is five years from now. Complete this application for yourself. List the type of job you might have. List the salary that you expect to be making. Decide what your marital status might be. Make up credit references. When you're finished, you will have a picture of yourself as a future credit applicant.

ELECTRIC AVENUE **GOLD 'N GEMS** **AutoExpress** **HOME IDEAS** **APPAREL**

Montgomery Ward
EXPRESS
credit

Source Code	Customer Waiting	Amount of Sale	Dept.
966		$	

For Office Use Only ▼

Credit Limit $		Sale Appr. $
Key #		
Acct. #		Expir. Date

FIRST NAME	INITIAL	LAST NAME	TITLE (JR,SR,ETC.)

PRESENT ADDRESS   STREET

CITY   STATE   ZIP

PREVIOUS ADDRESS   (IF LESS THAN TWO YEARS AT PRESENT ADDRESS)   CITY   STATE   ZIP

DATE OF BIRTH / /	SOC. SEC. NO. / /	HOME PHONE ( )	BUSINESS PHONE ( )

EMPLOYER	HOW LONG	ANNUAL INCOME*	OCCUPATION

NO. DEPENDENTS
- ☐ OWN   ☐ BOARD –
- ☐ RENT   LIVE W/RELATIVE(S)

HOW LONG (YEARS)   MORTGAGE/RENT PAYMENT

HAVE YOU EVER HAD A MONTGOMERY WARD CHARGE CARD?
- ☐ NO   ACCT.
- ☐ YES   **NO.**

CREDIT REFERENCES

☐ CHECKING   ☐ SAVINGS   ☐ VISA   ☐ MASTERCARD   ☐ SEARS/DISCOVER   ☐ AMERICAN EXPRESS/OPTIMA   ☐ DEPT. STORE

PLEASE COMPLETE FOR CO-APPLICANT OR AUTHORIZED USER

FIRST NAME	INITIAL	LAST NAME	TITLE (JR,SR,ETC.)

PRESENT ADDRESS   (IF DIFFERENT THAN ABOVE)   CITY   STATE   ZIP

ANNUAL INCOME*	SOC. SEC. NO. / /	RELATIONSHIP TO APPLICANT
		☐ SPOUSE ☐ OTHER

Co-Applicant must sign Agreement. If individual listed above is Co-Applicant, check box ☐

*Alimony, Child Support or Separate Maintenance Payments Need Not Be Disclosed Unless Relied Upon for Credit

I desire Montgomery Ward Credit Security Plan Insurance on my Montgomery Ward credit accounts as described in the brochure furnished me and in accordance with the terms stated in the Certificates of Insurance to be sent. The cost is 50¢ per $100 (AZ 57¢, CA 48.6¢***, IL 82.9¢/85¢*, MD 51.5¢/50¢*, MT 70¢, NM 75¢**, NV 85.9¢/69¢*, OH 67¢/57¢*, OR 75¢***, VA 48¢**) of my previous balance each month. This insurance is voluntary, it may be obtained through a person of my choosing (in IL, CSP property insurance pays first but may limit recovery from similar coverages) and I may cancel at any time.

　*First rate to age 66: second rate at and after 66.
　**Not available age 70 and older.
　***Not available age 65 and older.

Holder Signature   **Age**

Yes, I accept your invitation to apply for a Montgomery Ward Credit Account and if I do not qualify, please consider this as an application for a Montgomery Ward Starter Account. I authorize you to verify the information concerning me in accordance with your established credit-policy. See reverse side for terms of both Accounts and legal disclosures.

X _____
Signature   Date

X _____
Signature   Date

37492-3 AZ, CA, DC, DE, IL, KY, MD, MT, NH, NM, NV, OH, OR, VA   REV. 7/91

SHOW WHAT YOU KNOW . . .

About Credit Applications

Obtain two different credit applications from local stores. Bring them to class and fill them out. Make up credit references and bank accounts, but use your own name, address, and phone number. Exchange completed forms with a classmate. Check each other's applications and make suggestions for improvement.

Installment purchases and loans

Making monthly installment payments is often easier than making one large payment. That is one reason people have credit cards. Sometimes people make expensive purchases. They may buy a refrigerator, a sofa, or new carpeting. They will pay for these things in monthly installments.

In order to pay for a college education, a car, or a house, many people borrow money from a bank, a credit union, or a finance company. When you apply for a loan, you will be asked the same type of information you are asked when you apply for a credit card. You also may be asked for more specific information. A creditor will look closely at these things:

- your *assets* (whether you own stocks or bonds, have a savings account, own a car)

- your *debts* (how much you pay out each month for other loans, credit cards, and so forth)

- your *work and salary history* (how long you have held your job and whether your job pays enough for you to make any new credit payments)

- your *credit references* (credit accounts you have paid up and how well you paid these accounts)

- the size of your *down payment* (On major purchases, such as cars, vans, homes, or campers, most applicants must make a cash payment.)

You need to remember that you will be charged for the privilege of paying monthly installments. A finance charge will be added to the unpaid balance of your credit card account. An interest charge will be added to the amount you repay on a loan.

ACTIVITY 13
Applying for a loan

Pretend that you need a student loan. Complete the application below. Make all your answers as realistic as you can.

LENDER COPY

GUARANTEED STUDENT LOAN (GSL) APPLICATION PROMISSORY NOTE

SECTION A - TO BE COMPLETED BY BORROWER (*PRINT IN INK—PRESS FIRMLY—OR TYPE*)

1. NAME (NO NICKNAMES)

LAST   FIRST   M I

2. SOCIAL SECURITY NUMBER

3. WHEN WERE YOU BORN? MO   DAY   YR

4. PERMANENT ADDRESS

5. PERMANENT HOME PHONE ( )

CITY   STATE   ZIP

6. U.S. CITIZENSHIP STATUS (CHECK ONE)
☐ U.S. CITIZEN OR NATIONAL   ☐ PERMANENT RESIDENT OR OTHER ELIGIBLE ALIEN

ALIEN ID NUMBER IF APPLICABLE

7. PERMANENT RESIDENT OF WHICH STATE

8a. DRIVER LICENSE NUMBER (IF YOU DO NOT HAVE A LICENSE, PRINT "NONE" AND GO TO 9)

8b STATE IN WHICH ISSUED

9. ADDRESS WHILE IN SCHOOL (STREET, CITY, STATE, ZIP)

10. PHONE AT SCHOOL ADDRESS ( )

11. MAJOR COURSE OF STUDY, SEE INSTRUCTIONS IN APP. BOOKLET

12. LOAN AMOUNT REQUESTED $ .00

13. LOAN PERIOD FROM MO YR TO MO YR

PRIOR LOAN INFORMATION

14. HAVE YOU EVER DEFAULTED ON A GSL, SLS (ALAS), PLUS, CONSOLIDATED, OR INCOME CONTINGENT LOAN?
☐ YES (GIVE DETAILS ON SEPARATE SHEET) ☐ NO

15a. DO YOU HAVE ANY PRIOR UNPAID GSL LOANS?
☐ YES (GO TO 15b) ☐ NO (GO TO 20a)

15b. IF YES, TOTAL UNPAID BALANCE OF GSL LOANS $

16. UNPAID PRINCIPAL BALANCE OF MOST RECENT GSL $

17. GRADE LEVEL OF MOST RECENT GSL, SEE INSTRUCTIONS IN APP. BOOKLET

18. LOAN PERIOD START DATE OF MOST RECENT GSL MO DAY YR

19. INTEREST RATE OF MOST RECENT GSL
☐ 7%   ☐ 8%   ☐ 9%

20a. DO YOU HAVE ANY PRIOR UNPAID SLS (ALAS) OR PLUS LOANS? ☐ YES (GO TO 20b) ☐ NO (GO TO 21a)

20b IF YES, TOTAL UNPAID PRINCIPAL BALANCE OF PRIOR SLS (ALAS) LOANS RECEIVED DURING ▶ UNDERGRADUATE STUDY $_____ GRADUATE STUDY $_____

21a. DO YOU HAVE ANY UNPAID PLUS LOANS IF YOU BORROWED AS A PARENT UNDER THE PLUS LOAN PROGRAM? ☐ YES (GO TO 21b) ☐ NO (GO TO 22a)

21b. IF YES, TOTAL PRINCIPAL BALANCE OF PLUS LOANS $

REFERENCES (YOU MUST PROVIDE THREE DIFFERENT NAMES, WITH DIFFERENT U.S. ADDRESSES AND PHONE NUMBERS)

PARENT GUARDIAN
22a. NAME _____
STREET _____
CITY, STATE, ZIP _____
PHONE ( )

RELATIVE
22b. NAME _____
STREET _____
CITY, STATE ZIP _____
PHONE ( )

RELATIVE
22c. NAME _____
STREET _____
CITY, STATE, ZIP _____
PHONE ( )

NOTICE TO BORROWER: You must read the additional Promissory Note terms and the Borrower's Certification on the reverse side before signing this Promissory Note. PROMISE TO PAY: I promise to pay to the order of my lender the entire Loan Amount Requested shown above, to the extent that it is advanced to me, including the Guarantee Fee and the Origination Fee and interest of the unpaid principal balance, subject to the terms and conditions described on the reverse side of this Promissory Note and to the terms and conditions contained in the Disclosure Statement that will be provided to me no later than the time of the first disbursement of this loan. I have read, I understand, and I agree to the Borrower's Certification on the reverse side of this Promissory Note. I understand that this is a Promissory Note. I will not sign it before reading all of its provisions, even if otherwise advised. I am entitled to a copy of this Promissory Note. By signing this Promissory Note I acknowledge that I have received an exact copy of it.

23a. SIGNATURE OF BORROWER (APPLICATION CANNOT BE PROCESSED WITHOUT SIGNATURE)
X

23b. DATE BORROWER SIGNED MO DAY YR

SECTION B - TO BE COMPLETED BY SCHOOL

24. NAME OF SCHOOL

26. PHONE ( )

27. SCHOOL CODE

25. ADDRESS (STREET, CITY, STATE, ZIP)

28.

29.

30. PERIOD LOAN WILL COVER FROM MO DAY YR TO MO DAY YR

31. STUDENT'S GRADE LEVEL (CHECK ONE)
CORRESP ☐0 UNDERGRAD ☐1 ☐2 ☐3 ☐4 ☐5 GRAD ☐6 ☐7 ☐8 ☐9 ☐10

32. ANTICIPATED GRADUATION DATE MO DAY YR

33. STUDENT STATUS (CHECK ONE) ☐ DEPENDENT ☐ INDEPENDENT

34. ADJUSTED GROSS INCOME (AGI) $

35. COST OF ATTENDANCE FOR LOAN PERIOD $

36. ESTIMATED FINANCIAL AID FOR LOAN PERIOD $

37. EXPECTED FAMILY CONTRIBUTION (EFC) $

38. DIFFERENCE (ITEM 35 LESS ITEMS 36 AND 37) OR LEGAL MAXIMUM $

39. SUGGESTED DISBURSEMENT DATES
1ST DISB. MO DAY YR
2ND DISB MO DAY YR
3RD DISB MO DAY YR

40. DO SUGGESTED DISBURSEMENT DATES CORRESPOND TO SCHOOL TERMS? YES ☐ NO ☐

41. WILL THE STUDENT ATTEND A FOREIGN SCHOOL? YES ☐ NO ☐

42. SCHOOL USE ONLY

I HAVE READ, I UNDERSTAND, AND I AGREE TO THE TERMS OF THE SCHOOL CERTIFICATION PRINTED ON THE REVERSE SIDE OF THIS APPLICATION.

43a. SIGNATURE OF SCHOOL OFFICIAL X

43b. DATE MO DAY YR

43c. PRINT NAME AND TITLE

SECTION C - TO BE COMPLETED BY LENDER

44. NAME OF LENDER

46. LENDER CODE

50. LOAN DISBURSEMENTS MO DAY YR $ AMOUNT

45. ADDRESS (STREET, BUILDING, CITY, STATE, ZIP)

47. BRANCH CODE

MO DAY YR $ AMOUNT

52. IS THIS AN UNSUBSIDIZED LOAN? YES ☐ NO ☐

53. LENDER ACCOUNT NUMBER

54. LENDER USE ONLY

48.

MO DAY YR $ AMOUNT

SECTION D - TO BE COMPLETED BY HEAF

55a. SIGNATURE OF LENDING OFFICIAL X
PRINT NAME AND TITLE

49.

51. TOTAL LOAN AMOUNT APPROVED $ .00

56. HEAF USE ONLY

57. PROMISSORY NOTE STATUS

55b. DATE SIGNED MO DAY YR

74

Order forms

When you order from a catalog, you need to know how to fill out an order form. Even if you are telephoning your order, it is helpful to fill out the order form before you make the call. You can refer to the order form as you give your order on the phone.

You will usually find space for the following information on an order form: number of the page showing the item you want, item number, description of item, and quantity. If you are ordering clothing, you will have to fill in color and size. You will also have to show the price of each item and figure shipping costs. In some states, you will have to add sales tax. Then you must total the amount owed.

ACTIVITY 14
Completing order forms

Below is a sample catalog page. On page 77 is a sample order form. The first item ordered is filled out for you. Add at least two items from the catalog page to the order form. Assume that the sales tax is 6 percent. Total the amount due.

Summer weight
100% cotton
short-sleeved shirts

Striped: green/white. blue/white. tan/white
S1147 Men's **$26.00**
S1148 Women's **$26.00**

Solid: plum, jade, khaki, gray, teal, white, mustard, chili
L4132 Men's **$25.00**
L4133 Women's **$25.00**

16 Men's neck sizes: S (14–14 $^1/_2$), M (15–15 $^1/_2$), L (16–16 $^1/_2$), XL (17–17 $^1/_2$)
Women's sizes: S (6–8), M (10–12), L (14–16), XL (18–20)

Athletic Shoes

Practical!
Built-in comfort!
Provides support
where needed!

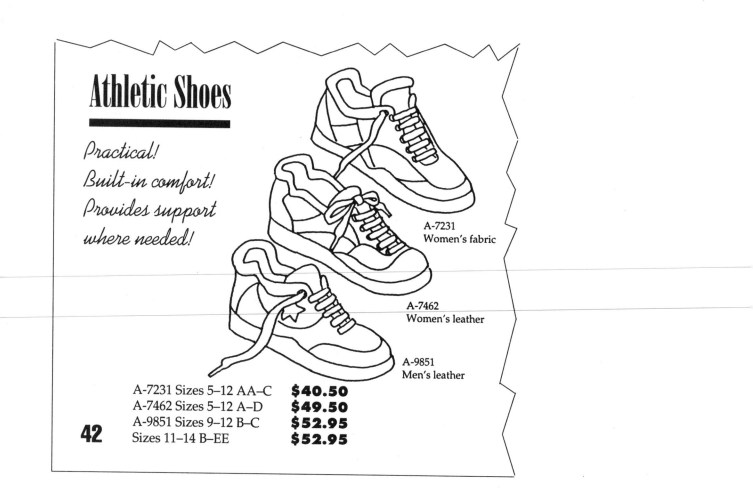

A-7231
Women's fabric

A-7462
Women's leather

A-9851
Men's leather

A-7231 Sizes 5–12 AA–C   **$40.50**
A-7462 Sizes 5–12 A–D   **$49.50**
A-9851 Sizes 9–12 B–C   **$52.95**
        Sizes 11–14 B–EE   **$52.95**

42

Lightweight nylon jacket

Sale!

- *Drawstring hood*
- *Elastic wrists*

Made in USA
Colors: Green or blue only

Men's and women's sizes:
M (38–40), L (42–44), XL (46–48)

46   J614NS   ~~$32.50~~   **Now: $17.95**

FOSTER & HARLEY
4 E. Main St.
Lake Edge, Indiana

Your Name _____

Address _____

_____
Street   Apt.

_____
City   State   ZIP

Day phone ( ) _____

Evening phone ( ) _____

Page	Item No.	Description	Color	Size	Qty.	Price	Total
16	S 1147	Men's Striped Shirt	Green/White	L	1	26.00	26.00

Shipping, Handling, & Insurance

If merchandise total is

up to $20	add $3.95
$20.01 to $40	add $4.95
$40.01 to $60	add $5.95
$60.01 to $80	add $6.95

Total Merchandise $ _____

Applicable Sales Tax $ _____

Shipping, Handling, & Insurance $ _____

Total Amt. Due $ _____

Please check your method of payment:

_____ Full payment enclosed—check or money order

_____ American Express _____ VISA _____ MasterCard _____ Discover

Account number _____ Expiration date: _____

SHOW WHAT YOU KNOW . . .

About Order Forms

Bring one or two catalogs with order forms to class. Fill out an order form and have another class member check your work and your arithmetic.

Filing a 1040EZ

adjusted gross income   total amount earned before any tax or other money is withheld

dependent   anyone who depends on another for support; a dependent may be a child, wife, husband, parent, or other relative

exemption   fixed amount that may be deductible for support of one or more dependents or oneself

filer   person who submits (files) a tax return

refund   money returned from the Internal Revenue Service or a state or provincial department of revenue because taxes were overpaid

standard deduction   fixed amount that may be subtracted from adjusted gross income

tax table   table in instruction booklet used to find out how much tax is owed

W-2 Form   a yearly statement from an employer showing what was earned and withheld; a wage and tax statement

withholding   money deducted or withheld from a paycheck by an employer

If you hold a paying job, you will probably have to report your wages, salary, and tips to the Internal Revenue Service (IRS) of your federal government. You may also have to report the same amounts to the revenue department of the state or province in which you live.

Before the deadline of April 15, taxpayers prepare a tax return reporting all income from the previous calendar year. U.S. federal tax form 1040EZ is a simple form for persons who are single and have no children. If you are filing a return for the first time, you can find tax forms at most post offices, libraries, and banks. If you have paid taxes before, tax forms and instructions will usually be mailed to you. (NOTE: Since tax forms and tax laws almost always change from year to year, you must read the instructions that accompany the form you file.)

ACTIVITY 15
Understanding income tax words

Match the tax words below with their meanings.

A	B
_____ 1. exemption	**A.** total amount you earned before anything was withheld
_____ 2. refund	**B.** person who submits a tax return
_____ 3. adjusted gross income	**C.** what your employer provides to show earnings and withholding
_____ 4. dependent	
_____ 5. W–2 Form	**D.** fixed amount you may deduct for support of dependents and self
_____ 6. tax table	**E.** fixed amount you may be able to deduct from adjusted gross income
_____ 7. standard deduction	
_____ 8. interest income	**F.** table showing what your taxes are
_____ 9. withholding	**G.** money you earned on a savings account
_____ 10. filer	**H.** money your employer deducted from your paycheck
	I. money the IRS owes you
	J. person who depends on you for support

ACTIVITY 16
Working with income tax words

Below is a story about Timothy J. Chen, a taxpayer. Fill in each of the missing terms from the list.

adjusted gross income	interest income	withheld
wages	W–2 Form	refund
return	dependent	tax table

Timothy J. Chen, a student who worked in 1992, had to file his first income tax _____ . Tim, who is sixteen, worked at Super Burger during the year. He earned $2,000 in _____ and no tips. The _____ on his savings account was $50. His _____ was $2,050. Since Tim's parents provided most of his support, they will be able to claim him as a _____ on their tax return. Tim's employer _____ a total of $40 in federal taxes from Tim's wages. Tim checked the _____ to see what taxes, if any, were owed. He found out that the IRS was overpaid by $31.

Tim will get a small _____ !

ACTIVITY 17
Using a 1040EZ

Look at the 1040EZ for Timothy J. Chen (p. 81). Part of the reverse side of the form is shown below. Answer the questions about Tim's return.

1. Tim checked —————————————————— for the Presidential Election Campaign.

2. Tim earned —————————————————— in wages in 1992.

3. Tim had interest income of —————————————————— .

4. Tim checked —————————————————— for line 4.

5. Look at the worksheet from the reverse side of 1040EZ. Is this worksheet completed correctly?

    ————————————————

6. On what line is Tim's refund shown? ——————————————————

1992   Instructions for Form 1040EZ

Use this form if
- Your filing status is single.
- You do not claim any dependents.
- You were under 65* and not blind at the end of 1992.
- Your taxable income (line 5) is less than $50,000.
- You had **only** wages, salaries, tips, and taxable scholarship or fellowship grants, and your taxable interest income was $400 or less. **Caution:** *If you earned tips, including allocated tips, that are not included in box 13 and box 14 of your W-2, you may not be able to use Form 1040EZ. See page 12 in the booklet. Also, you cannot use this form if you had more than one employer and your total wages were over $55,500.*
- You did not receive any advance earned income credit payments.
- * *If you turned 65 on January 1, 1993, you are considered to be age 65 at the end of 1992.*

If you are not sure about your filing status, see page 6 in the booklet. If you have questions about dependents, see Tele-Tax (topic no. 155) on page 20 in the booklet.

If you can't use this form, see Tele-Tax (topic no. 152) on page 20 in the booklet.

Filling in your return

Please print your numbers inside the boxes. Do not type your numbers. Do not use dollar signs.

Most people can fill in the form by following the instructions on the front. But you will have to use the booklet if you received a scholarship or fellowship grant or tax-exempt interest income, such as on municipal bonds. Also, use the booklet if you received a Form 1099-INT showing income tax withheld (backup withholding).

Remember, you must report your wages, salaries, and tips even if you don't get a W-2 form from your employer. You must also report all your taxable interest income, including interest from savings accounts at banks, savings and loans, credit unions, etc., even if you don't get a Form 1099-INT.

If you paid someone to prepare your return, that person must also sign it and show other information. See page 15 in the booklet.

Department of the Treasury—Internal Revenue Service

Form 1040EZ

Income Tax Return for Single Filers With No Dependents (L) **1992**

OMB No. 1545-0675

Name & address

Use the IRS label (see page 10). If you don't have one, please print.

L A B E L   H E R E

Print your name (first, initial, last)
Timothy J. Chen

Home address (number and street). If you have a P.O. box, see page 10.   Apt. no.
885 Scott Street

City, town or post office, state, and ZIP code. If you have a foreign address, see page 10.
Anytown, MD 01234

Please see instructions on the back. Also, see the Form 1040EZ booklet.

Please print your numbers like this:

9 8 7 6 5 4 3 2 1 0

Your social security number

000 00 0000

Presidential Election Campaign (See page 10.)
Do you want $1 to go to this fund?

Note: Checking "Yes" will not change your tax or reduce your refund. ▶

Yes No
[✓]

| | Dollars | Cents |

Report your income

Attach Copy B of Form(s) W-2 here. Attach tax payment on top of Form(s) W-2.

Note: *You must check Yes or No.*

1 Total wages, salaries, and tips. This should be shown in box 10 of your W-2 form(s). Attach your W-2 form(s). 1	2,000	00
2 Taxable interest income of $400 or less. If the total is more than $400, you cannot use Form 1040EZ. 2	50	00
3 Add lines 1 and 2. This is your **adjusted gross income.** 3	2,050	00
4 Can your parents (or someone else) claim you on their return? [✓] **Yes.** Do worksheet on back; enter amount from line E here. [ ] **No.** Enter 5,900.00. This is the total of your standard deduction and personal exemption. 4	2,000	00
5 Subtract line 4 from line 3. If line 4 is larger than line 3, enter 0. This is your **taxable income.** 5	50	00

Figure your tax

6 Enter your Federal income tax withheld from box 9 of your W-2 form(s). 6	40	00
7 **Tax.** Look at line 5 above. Use the amount on **line 5** to find your tax in the tax table on pages 22–24 of the booklet. Then, enter the tax from the table on this line. 7	9	00

Refund or amount you owe

8 If line 6 is larger than line 7, subtract line 7 from line 6. This is your **refund.** 8	31	00
9 If line 7 is larger than line 6, subtract line 6 from line 7. This is the **amount you owe.** Attach your payment for full amount payable to the "Internal Revenue Service." Write your name, address, social security number, daytime phone number, and "1992 Form 1040EZ" on it. 9		

Sign your return

Keep a copy of this form for your records.

I have read this return. Under penalties of perjury, I declare that to the best of my knowledge and belief, the return is true, correct, and complete.

Your signature
X *Timothy J. Chen*

Date
2-14-93

Your occupation
server

For IRS Use Only – Please do not write in boxes below.

[ ] [ ] [ ] [ ]

[ ] [ ] [ ] [ ]

For Privacy Act and Paperwork Reduction Act Notice, see page 4 in the booklet.   Cat. No. 12617R   Form 1040EZ (1992)

Filing a 1040A

Many taxpayers use Form 1040A. This return is for both married and single persons. On Tim Chen's 1040EZ, he reported income from wages and interest income. On the 1040A, taxpayers also report dividends, IRA distributions, unemployment compensation, and other sources of income. This form allows for certain tax credits, such as credit for child and dependent care expenses. A parent who works may qualify for earned income credit.

The activities that follow deal with the 1040A. Become familiar with the 1040A "Words to Know" before beginning these activities.

ACTIVITY 18
Working with income tax words

Complete the statements about John and Lisa Chen's income tax return. The couple is filing a joint return using Form 1040A. Fill in each of the missing terms from the list.

dependent   IRA
refund   unemployment compensation
joint return   dividends
exemptions   tax-exempt
interest income   withheld

Because John and Lisa Chen are married, they are filing a _____ using 1040A. They will claim son Timothy as a _____. They can claim themselves as _____ .

In addition to the salaries that both Chens earn, they also receive _____ from a savings account and _____ from investments in the stock market. However, some of the interest they receive is _____ , meaning they don't have to pay federal taxes on that interest. Since neither of the Chens was out of work, they will not have to show _____ .

Neither John nor Lisa received any payments made from an individual retirement arrangement known as an _____ . Since Lisa and John have already had money_____ from their pay checks, they are hoping to get a _____ this year.

83

ACTIVITY 19
Using 1040A

The Chens used the fifteen steps outlined in their instruction booklet for 1040A to help complete their return. The final return appears on the next two pages. Review the information for both pages before completing the statements below.

1. Do John and Lisa want $1 to go to the Presidential Election Campaign Fund? _____

2. Which filing status is checked on the return? _____

3. Is box 6a checked? _____

4. Who is Timothy J. Chen? _____

5. How many exemptions did the Chens claim? _____

6. What is the total income of both John and Lisa? _____

7. How much taxable interest income did they have? _____

8. Did they have any tax-exempt interest? _____

9. On what line are dividends shown? _____

10. Did the Chens add their total income correctly? _____

11. Did they have any IRA distributions? _____

12. Do the Chens qualify for "Earned income credit"? _____

13. Did the Chens enter the correct standard deduction on line 19? _____

14. What is the amount entered on line 21? _____

15. What is the Chens' taxable income? _____

16. Did the Chens use the tax table? _____

17. The total tax for the Chens is on line _____ .

18. Total federal income tax withheld is on line _____ .

19. Do the Chens owe money? _____

20. Did the Chens prepare their own return? _____

Form **1040A**	Department of the Treasury—Internal Revenue Service **U.S. Individual Income Tax Return** (L)	**1992**	IRS Use Only—Do not write or staple in this space.

OMB No. 1545-0085

Label
(See page 14.)

Use the IRS label. Otherwise, please print or type.

Your first name and initial — John T.   Last name — Chen

Your social security number — 000 00 0000

If a joint return, spouse's first name and initial — Lisa M.   Last name — Chen

Spouse's social security number — 000 00 0000

Home address (number and street). If you have a P.O. box, see page 15. — 885 Scott Street   Apt. no.

For Privacy Act and Paperwork Reduction Act Notice, see page 4.

City, town or post office, state, and ZIP code. If you have a foreign address, see page 15. — Anytown, MD 01234

Presidential Election Campaign Fund (See page 15.)   Yes | No

Do you want $1 to go to this fund? . . . . — ✔

If a joint return, does your spouse want $1 to go to this fund? — ✔

Note: *Checking "Yes" will not change your tax or reduce your refund.*

Check the box for your filing status
(See page 15.)

Check only one box.

1 ☐ Single

2 ☒ Married filing joint return (even if only one had income)

3 ☐ Married filing separate return. Enter spouse's social security number above and full name here. ▶ _____

4 ☐ Head of household (with qualifying person). (See page 16.) If the qualifying person is a child but not your dependent, enter this child's name here. ▶ _____

5 ☐ Qualifying widow(er) with dependent child (year spouse died ▶ 19 ___). (See page 17.)

Figure your exemptions
(See page 18.)

If more than seven dependents, see page 21.

6a ☒ **Yourself.** If your parent (or someone else) can claim you as a dependent on his or her tax return, do not check box 6a. But be sure to check the box on line 18b on page 2.

b ☐ **Spouse**

No. of boxes checked on 6a and 6b	2

c Dependents:

(1) Name (first, initial, and last name)	(2) Check if under age 1	(3) If age 1 or older, dependent's social security number	(4) Dependent's relationship to you	(5) No. of months lived in your home in 1992
Timothy S. Chen	✔	: :	son	12
		: :		
		: :		
		: :		
		: :		
		: :		

No. of your children on 6c who:

• lived with you — 1

• didn't live with you due to divorce or separation (see page 21) — ___

No. of other dependents on 6c — ___

d If your child didn't live with you but is claimed as your dependent under a pre-1985 agreement, check here . . . . ▶ ☐

e Total number of exemptions claimed.

Add numbers entered on lines above	3

Figure your total income

Attach Copy B of your Forms W-2 and 1099-R here.

If you didn't get a W-2, see page 22.

Attach check or money order on top of any Forms W-2 or 1099-R.

7 Wages, salaries, tips, etc. This should be shown in box 10 of your W-2 form(s). Attach Form(s) W-2.   7   48,672 00

8a Taxable interest income (see page 24). If over $400, also complete and attach Schedule 1, Part I.   8a   180 00

b Tax-exempt interest. DO NOT include on line 8a.   8b   75

9 Dividends. If over $400, also complete and attach Schedule 1, Part II.   9   47 00

10a Total IRA distributions.   10a   10b Taxable amount (see page 25).   10b

11a Total pensions and annuities.   11a   11b Taxable amount (see page 25).   11b

12 Unemployment compensation (see page 29).   12

13a Social security benefits.   13a   13b Taxable amount (see page 29).   13b

14 Add lines 7 through 13b (far right column). This is your **total income.** ▶   14   48,899 00

Figure your adjusted gross income

15a Your IRA deduction from applicable worksheet.   15a

b Spouse's IRA deduction from applicable worksheet. **Note:** *Rules for IRAs begin on page 31.*   15b

c Add lines 15a and 15b. These are your **total adjustments.**   15c

16 Subtract line 15c from line 14. This is your **adjusted gross income.** If less than $22,370, see "Earned income credit" on page 39. ▶   16   48,899 00

Cat. No. 12601H

1992 Form 1040A page 1

Name(s) shown on page 1.	Your social security number
John T. & Lisa M. Chen	000 00 0000

Figure your standard deduction, exemption amount, and taxable income	17	Enter the amount from line 16.	17	48,899	00
	18a	Check if: ☐ You were 65 or older ☐ Blind ☐ Spouse was 65 or older ☐ Blind } Enter number of boxes checked ▶ 18a			
	b	If your parent (or someone else) can claim you as a dependent, check here . . . . ▶ 18b ☐			
	c	If you are married filing separately and your spouse files Form 1040 and itemizes deductions, see page 35 and check here ▶ 18c ☐			
	19	Enter the **standard deduction** shown below for your filing status. **But if you checked any box on line 18a or b,** go to page 35 to find your standard deduction. **If you checked box 18c,** enter -0-. • Single—$3,600 • Head of household—$5,250 • Married filing jointly or Qualifying widow(er)—$6,000 • Married filing separately—$3,000	19	6,000	00
	20	Subtract line 19 from line 17. (If line 19 is more than line 17, enter -0-.)	20	42,899	00
	21	Multiply $2,300 by the total number of exemptions claimed on line 6e.	21	6,900	00
	22	Subtract line 21 from line 20. (If line 21 is more than line 20, enter -0-.) This is your **taxable income.** ▶	22	35,999	00

Figure your tax, credits, and payments If you want the IRS to figure your tax, see the instructions for line 22 on page 36.	23	Find the tax on the amount on line 22. Check if from: ☐ Tax Table (pages 48–53) or ☐ Form 8615 (see page 37).	23	5,419	00
	24a	Credit for child and dependent care expenses. Complete and attach Schedule 2. 24a			
	b	Credit for the elderly or the disabled. Complete and attach Schedule 3. 24b			
	c	Add lines 24a and 24b. These are your **total credits.**	24c		
	25	Subtract line 24c from line 23. (If line 24c is more than line 23, enter -0-.)	25		
	26	Advance earned income credit payments from Form W-2.	26		
	27	Add lines 25 and 26. This is your **total tax.** ▶	27	5,419	00
	28a	Total Federal income tax withheld. If any tax is from Form(s) 1099, check here. ▶ ☐ 28a 6,841 00			
	b	1992 estimated tax payments and amount applied from 1991 return. 28b			
	c	**Earned income credit.** Complete and attach Schedule EIC. 28c			
	d	Add lines 28a, 28b, and 28c. These are your **total payments.** ▶	28d	6,841	00

Figure your refund or amount you owe Attach check or money order on top of Form(s) W-2, etc., on page 1.	29	If line 28d is more than line 27, subtract line 27 from line 28d. This is the amount you **overpaid.**	29		
	30	Amount of line 29 you want **refunded to you.**	30	1,422	00
	31	Amount of line 29 you want **applied to your 1993 estimated tax.** 31			
	32	If line 27 is more than line 28d, subtract line 28d from line 27. This is the **amount you owe.** Attach check or money order for full amount payable to the "Internal Revenue Service". Write your name, address, social security number, daytime phone number, and "1992 Form 1040A" on it.	32		
	33	Estimated tax penalty (see page 41). 33			

Sign your return Keep a copy of this return for your records.	Under penalties of perjury, I declare that I have examined this return and accompanying schedules and statements, and to the best of my knowledge and belief, they are true, correct, and complete. Declaration of preparer (other than the taxpayer) is based on all information of which the preparer has any knowledge.		
	Your signature *John T. Chen*	Date 2-15-93	Your occupation sales assistant
	Spouse's signature. If joint return, BOTH must sign. *Lisa M. Chen*	Date 2-15-93	Spouse's occupation Receptionist

Paid preparer's use only	Preparer's signature ▶	Date	Check if self-employed ☐	Preparer's social security no.
	Firm's name (or yours if self-employed) and address ▶		E.I. No.	
			ZIP code	

☆ U.S. GOVERNMENT PRINTING OFFICE: 1992 315-035

Below you will find profiles of two different taxpayers. Each one has chosen the 1040EZ return. Pretend you are one of these persons. Complete the 1040EZ on the next page for the person you select.

PROFILE: Tracy E. Alexander

SS# - 574-22-2364

Age - 16

Occupation - Student/Part-time Stock Person

Marital Status - Single

Tracy lives at 886 George Street in St. Albans, West Virginia. The ZIP Code is 25314. Tracy's W-2 Form showed $2,350.17 in gross income. Federal taxes paid were $72. Tracy:

1. Has no children and no other dependents
2. Will be claimed on parents' return
3. Earned $36 in interest income

The tax table shows $6 due on Tracy's income.

PROFILE: Jackie Fletcher

SS# - 584-01-1775

Age - 23

Occupation - Secretary

Marital Status - Single

Jackie lives at 8134 C Street, Apt. E-13, in Raleigh, North Carolina. The ZIP Code is 27609. Jackie lives alone and earns about $200 per week. This year's W-2 Form shows $975 paid in federal taxes and $11,020 in gross income. Jackie:

1. Has no children or other dependents
2. Earned $380 in interest income

The tax table shows $829 due on Jackie's taxable income.

Form **1040EZ**

Department of the Treasury—Internal Revenue Service

Income Tax Return for
Single Filers With No Dependents (L) **1992**

' OMB No. 1545-0675

Name & address

Use the IRS label (see page 10). If you don't have one, please print.

L A B E L   H E R E

Print your name (first, initial, last)

Home address (number and street). If you have a P.O. box, see page 10.   Apt. no.

City, town or post office, state, and ZIP code. If you have a foreign address, see page 10.

Please see instructions on the back. Also, see the Form 1040EZ booklet.

Please print your numbers like this:

9 8 7 6 5 4 3 2 1 0

Your social security number

Presidential Election Campaign (See page 10.)
Do you want $1 to go to this fund?

Note: *Checking "Yes" will not change your tax or reduce your refund.* ▶

Yes   No

Dollars   Cents

Report your income

Attach Copy B of Form(s) W-2 here. Attach tax payment on top of Form(s) W-2.

Note: *You must check Yes or No.*

1 Total wages, salaries, and tips. This should be shown in box 10 of your W-2 form(s). Attach your W-2 form(s). **1**

2 Taxable interest income of $400 or less. If the total is more than $400, you cannot use Form 1040EZ. **2**

3 Add lines 1 and 2. This is your **adjusted gross income.** **3**

4 Can your parents (or someone else) claim you on their return?
☐ **Yes.** Do worksheet on back; enter amount from line E here.
☐ **No.** Enter 5,900.00. This is the total of your standard deduction and personal exemption. **4**

5 Subtract line 4 from line 3. If line 4 is larger than line 3, enter 0. This is your **taxable income.** **5**

Figure your tax

6 Enter your Federal income tax withheld from box 9 of your W-2 form(s). **6**

7 **Tax.** Look at line 5 above. Use the amount on **line 5** to find your tax in the tax table on pages 22-24 of the booklet. Then, enter the tax from the table on this line. **7**

Refund or amount you owe

8 If line 6 is larger than line 7, subtract line 7 from line 6. This is your **refund.** **8**

9 If line 7 is larger than line 6, subtract line 6 from line 7. This is the **amount you owe.** Attach your payment for full amount payable to the "Internal Revenue Service." Write your name, address, social security number, daytime phone number, and "1992 Form 1040EZ" on it. **9**

Sign your return

Keep a copy of this form for your records.

I have read this return. Under penalties of perjury, I declare that to the best of my knowledge and belief, the return is true, correct, and complete.

Your signature   Date

X

Your occupation

For IRS Use Only - Please do not write in boxes below.

For Privacy Act and Paperwork Reduction Act Notice, see page 4 in the booklet.   Cat. No. 12617R   Form **1040EZ** (1992)

ANSWER KEY

Getting a Job

ACTIVITY 1—Making a Personal Fact Sheet (p. 3)
Fact sheets will vary but should include the kinds of information in the sample on p. 2.

ACTIVITY 2—Writing a Detailed Job Resume (p. 6)
Resumes will vary but should include personal information (name, address, phone number), educational background, employment history, special skills, special interests, and references.

ACTIVITY 3—Writing a Brief Resume (p. 7)
Resumes will vary but should include personal information, the position applied for, experience, education, and references. They should be no more than one page long.

ACTIVITY 4—Understanding Letters of Application (p. 8)
1. secretarial
2. Personnel Director
3. three years of secretarial training with typing and shorthand speeds of 60 and 120 words per minute; two years work experience as a part-time secretary
4. to talk with Mr. Benawra about a secretarial position in the main office of the Superior Manufacturing Company
5. by writing him at 126 Rockford Street, Chinaville, Ohio 44507, or calling 555-8181
6. a resume
7. part-time secretary for two years
8. yes; Malcolm X High School
9. 60 words per minute
10. 126 Rockford Street, Chinaville, Ohio 44507

SHOW WHAT YOU KNOW… About Letters of Application (p. 10)
Letters will vary. They should be in proper business letter format and include a statement of interest in a specific position, a brief statement of abilities (including a reference to the enclosed resume), and information about how and where the student can be reached.

ACTIVITY 5—Filling Out Job Applications (p. 11)
1. stock worker
2. L.A. High School
3. vocational
4. no
5. typewriter
6. stock
7. full time
8. no
9. no
10. no; the employer did not check the box preceding weight

ACTIVITY 6—Understanding a Job Application Form (p. 13)
Answers will vary. All information except signature should be printed.
1. today's date
2. name, last name first; social security number
3. address should include ZIP Code
4. If address in number 3 is temporary, permanent address including ZIP Code should be printed here; if address in number 3 is permanent, "Same" should be printed here.
5. phone number
6. job title, when student can start, and pay expected
7. "Yes" or "No" to indicate whether or not they are working; indicate if present employers can be contacted
8. Students should indicate if they have ever worked for the company and print the dates.
9. schools attended, graduation dates, and subjects studied (where appropriate)
10. any special subjects studied
11. any military service, including ranks
12. any clubs that do not indicate race, beliefs, or national origin
13. work experience (starting with last job first), the address of the company, salary, position, and reason for leaving
14. Students should list three adults not related to them and include full addresses and how long they have known each.
15. Students should list any major injuries or handicaps that may have an impact on their work performance.

16. Students should list a person who can be contacted in case of emergency and include the full address and phone number.
17. (There is no answer.)
18. today's date; name signed (not printed)

ACTIVITY—7 Filling Out Job Applications (p. 16)
The answers on the McDonald's form and the general form will vary. Students should print clearly and fill out the forms completely. It may be helpful to prepare a list of possible jobs for students to consider.

The McDonald's form includes a W–4 withholding allowance form that should be completed as fully as possible. Students probably will claim only one allowance on line 4, unless they are married or have dependent children. Students whose incomes are very low or who are full-time students may claim exemption from withholding.

Check Your Understanding of Job Application Forms (p. 21)
1. Answers will vary.
2. usually, the most recent
3. an employer who offers equal chances for employment to all applicants regardless of race, sex, creed, or national origin
4. church membership
5. a temporary or current address as opposed to a person's regular, long-term address
6. a necessary (legal) job requirement or qualification
7. you may lose your job without having been notified in advance; an employer reserves the right to fire you
8. race, sex, age, creed, national origin (any three of these)
9. Answers will vary. Students who are very concerned about neatness and showing that they can follow directions properly may request a new form. Students who believe they can correct the form neatly may choose not to request a new form.
10. personal information, employment desired, education, former employers, references (any three of these or similar responses)

SHOW WHAT YOU KNOW… About Job Application Forms (p. 21)
Answers will vary.

ACTIVITY 8—Preparing for a Job Interview (p. 23)
Answers will vary.

ACTIVITY 9—Preparing for a Job Interview (p. 23)
Answers will vary but may include some of the following:
1. **Like:** The applicant will be able to get to work easily and on time.
Dislike: The interviewer may feel that the applicant is more interested in the location than in the position.
2. **Like:** The interviewer may appreciate the applicant's honesty.
Dislike: The interviewer may wonder why the applicant couldn't get along with the former boss or how well the applicant will fit in.
3. **Like:** The interviewer may appreciate the applicant's honesty and willingness to work overtime on some days.
Dislike: The interviewer may wonder about the applicant's priorities.
4. **Like:** The interviewer may appreciate the applicant's honesty or feel that an applicant who really needs a job would be a good candidate.
Dislike: The interviewer may feel that the applicant is not focused enough about what he or she wants to do and will not be dedicated to the job.
5. **Like:** Unless the interviewer is a tennis fan, he or she is not likely to be satisfied with this answer. However, if the position is not yet available, this might be an acceptable answer.
Dislike: The interviewer may wonder about the applicant's priorities.

ACTIVITY 10—Preparing for a Job Interview (p. 24)
1. c
2. c
3. c
4. c
5. b

6. c

7. b

8. c

Check Your Understanding of Job Interviews (p. 26)

1. F
2. T (for most jobs)
3. F
4. F
5. F
6. Answers will vary. The answer should focus on the applicant's desire for more growth, responsibility, or training, rather than on the conflict with the former boss.
7. Answers will vary. The answer should focus on the fact that regular transportation is available or has already been arranged.
8. Answers will vary. The answer should include an apology for the inconvenience of the delay and a promise that the applicant will not be late again.
9. Answers will vary. As in question 6, the answer should focus on the applicant's desire for growth, rather than on the conflict.
10. Answers will vary. The answer should be more specific than the example, explaining either why the applicant needs a job or why the applicant chose this company to apply to.

SHOW WHAT YOU KNOW... About Job Interviews (p. 27)
Role plays will vary.

ACTIVITY 11—Telephoning about a Job (p. 30)

Ad #1
The first response is unsuitable. The ad clearly reads "Wanted—High School Students."

The second response is unsuitable. Although at first this response may appear to be suitable, a close reading of the ad will show that the applicant is free to request more information about the job over the phone. A specific question about the job would be more appropriate.

The third response is suitable. This is an appropriate response to "Call 555-7013 for information." The applicant does want more information and is requesting how to go about getting it.

Ad #2
The first response is suitable. The applicant waits until he or she reaches ext. 481 to ask for someone who would know something about the tutoring job. The applicant also identifies the paper where the ad appeared.

The second response is suitable. Although many employers will not discuss pay over the phone, this is a suitable question for this ad. Since the employer has not given a specific job location or the name of a person to contact, the applicant is justified in trying to get more information over the phone. The applicant was correct in waiting to reach ext. 481 with this question.

The third response is unsuitable. The ad specifically reads, "Nights." The employer is asking that each applicant screen himself or herself before calling.

The fourth response is unsuitable. The switchboard operator is the wrong person to ask.

The fifth response is suitable. This request is precise and concise. The applicant recognizes from the ad that 555-6130 is a switchboard. He or she must give an extension number.

ACTIVITY 12—Evaluating Telephone Interviews (p. 32)

Ad #1
1. Answers will vary.
2. The applicant achieved goal #1, but the applicant *did not* achieve goal #2. The employer merely wants to schedule interviews in advance. No salary information will be given out over the phone.

Ad #2
1. Answers will vary.
2. Yes, the applicant achieved her goal. She made the interviewer (Anne Hutchinson) aware of her qualifications and accepted the time suggested by the interviewer without hesitation.

ACTIVITY 13—Taking Phone Messages (p. 36)

IMPORTANT MESSAGE
FOR *Mr. Baker*
DATE *today's date* TIME *9:40* AM/PM
M *Robert Whitney*
OF *Baker + Bailey Law Firm*
PHONE *555-0703*

TELEPHONED	✓	PLEASE CALL	
CAME TO SEE YOU		WILL CALL AGAIN	✓
WANTS TO SEE YOU		RUSH	
RETURNED YOUR CALL		SPECIAL ATTENTION	

MESSAGE *He wants to discuss a case you are handling for him. Please call him tomorrow at home if he does not reach you today at 2 pm*
SIGNED *(Student's name)*

TOPS ® FORM 3002P

IMPORTANT MESSAGE
FOR *John Penn*
DATE *today's date* TIME *3:30* AM/PM
M *Arnold Jenkins*
OF *Whitney Electronics*
PHONE *304 - 252-0401 21*

TELEPHONED	✓	PLEASE CALL	
CAME TO SEE YOU		WILL CALL AGAIN	
WANTS TO SEE YOU		RUSH	
RETURNED YOUR CALL		SPECIAL ATTENTION	

MESSAGE *He will have the information you requested tomorrow at 9 am*

SIGNED *J.J.*

TOPS ® FORM 3002P

Check Your Understanding of Telephone Skills (p. 39)
1–5 Answers will vary. Some examples:
1. "Mr. Greene is out of the office. May I help you?"
2. "Hello. I am calling about the part-time job at Burger Barn that was advertised in the *Tribune*."
3. "Hello. This is (student's name). I am calling for Mr. Greene, of Northwest Industries. Mr. Greene would like to make an appointment with you on either Monday or Tuesday morning of next week. Mr. Greene has told me that you are expecting a call from him about the appointment."
4. "Hello. I am calling about the part-time warehouse job you have recently advertised. I need to know if after-school hours are available."
5. "Hello. I would like to inquire about a part-time job as a sales clerk. Will you please tell me if you have any openings?"

SHOW WHAT YOU KNOW... About Telephone Skills (p. 40)
Role plays will vary.

ACTIVITY 14—Reading Want Ad Abbreviations (p. 42)
1. g **2.** f **3.** a **4.** c **5.** j **6.** b **7.** d **8.** i **9.** h **10.** e

ACTIVITY 15—Reading Want Ad Abbreviations (p. 42)
1. Apartment Manager
   Experienced for new high-rise building. Salary, apartment, and incentives.
2. Secretary
   For appliance store. Answer phone, file, no experience necessary, but must type 60 words per minute.
3. Fitters
   5 years experience. Good wages and benefits.

4. Die Makers
   Day work. Full benefits.
5. Quality Control Assistant
   Two years experience required in automotive. Good wages, benefits.
6. Lab Technician
   All-around plate man. Permanent position, excellent conditions and salary.

SHOW WHAT YOU KNOW... About Help-Wanted Ads (p. 44)
Answers will vary.

ACTIVITY 16—Reading Want Ads for Information (p. 45)
1. dishwasher, pizza maker
2. 222 Lane St.; 2:30–5:30 P.M.
3. Acme Personnel
4. 555-9683
5. hard shoes

ACTIVITY 17—Looking for Specific Jobs in the Want Ads (p. 45)
Ads and answers will vary.

ACTIVITY 181—Using the Help-Wanted Section of the Newspaper (p. 46)
1. 555-7870
2. one
3. Box C-1605, Local Press, Springfield
4. 555-6801
5. Stock Person (Arcade Attendant and Cashier ads also acceptable)
6. Job Finders, Inc.

Check Your Understanding of Help-Wanted Ads (p. 47)
1. experienced
2. assistant
3. preferred
4. salary
5. secretary
6. education
7. part-time
8. weekly
9. trainee
10. department
11. c
12. c
13. c
14. a
15. b

Filling Out Forms

ACTIVITY 1—Understanding the Vocabulary of Everyday Forms (p. 49)
1. C 2. F 3. G 4. I 5. D 6. B 7. H 8. J 9. A 10. E
11. revoked/suspended
12. valid
13. in lieu of
14. naturalized
15. mandatory

ACTIVITY 2—Completing Forms (p. 52)
Library Card Applications/Request for Information
Answers will vary.
ACTIVITY 3—Voter Registration Forms (p. 53)
1. Lance Adam Patterson
2. vote
3. 803 Long Lake Road, Elizabeth (New Jersey); Union
4. new registration
5. Vaughn P. Jonas

ACTIVITY 4—Filling Out an Application for a Social Security Card (p. 55)
1. T 2. T 3. F 4. T 5. T

Check Your Understanding of Forms (p. 57)
Answers will vary. The instructions for filling out the social security application are found on p. 55 of the student text. If students do not already have social security numbers, encourage them to complete an actual form, available at their local social security office.

SHOW WHAT YOU KNOW... About Forms (p. 57)
Answers will vary.

ACTIVITY 5—Filling in the "Dollars" Line (p. 60)

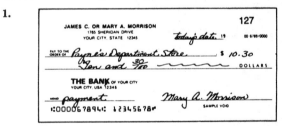

ACTIVITY 6—Writing Checks (p. 60)

1.
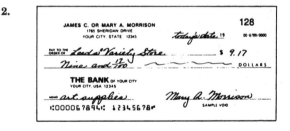

2.

3.

(Note: Students may also sign checks "James C. Morrison.")

ACTIVITY 7—Filling Out a Deposit Slip (p.62)
1. $10
2. September 15, 1994
3. no
4. two; $101.38; $10.00
5. 1-234-5678

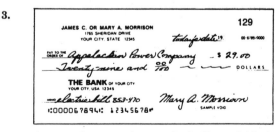

91

ACTIVITY 8—Keeping a Checkbook Register (p. 64)
1. $500
2. Montgomery Ward
3. July 16
4. a scarf
5. $440
6. Dr. Altchek
7. $387.50
8. August 14
9. $370
10. 868

ACTIVITY 9—Keeping a Checkbook Register (p.65)

NUMBER	DATE	DESCRIPTION OF TRANSACTION	PAYMENT/DEBIT (−)	√	FEE IF ANY (−)	DEPOSIT/CREDIT (+)	BALANCE	
							300	00
201		Myrtle's Daycare	35 00				265	00
202		Lim's Drugs	15 82				249	18
203		Jackson's Dept Store	21 00				228	18
204		Consumer's Power	46 82				181	36
205		Carson's Boutique	56 94				124	42
206		Ned's Place	48 52				75	90
		Cash Deposit				400 00	475	90

(Date column should show today's date for each check
and deposit recorded.)

ACTIVITY 10—Reading a Monthly Statement (p. 66)
1. checks 2. July 15; August 14 3. $500 4. $460 5. checks
6. deposit 7. $50 8. 22

Check Your Understanding of Bank Forms (p. 67)
1. Three and 44/100 ———
2. Forty-three and 53/100 ———
3. Two hundred seven and 0/100 ———
4. Seven hundred sixty-four and 5/100 ———
5. Twenty-five and 02/100 ———
6. b 7. c 8. a 9. b 10. a

ACTIVITY 11—Filling Out An Application for a Credit Card (p. 70)
1. Charles E. Wright 2. two 3. yes 4. renting an apartment 5. yes;
Harford Company 6. $2,500 7. $2,000 8. yes; yes; no
9. Frances Wright 10. Smith's Clothing 11. spouse of Charles
Wright 12. teacher 13. yes 14. Answers will vary.

ACTIVITY 12—Completing Credit Card Applications (p. 71)
Information on applications will vary. All information except signature
should be printed.

SHOW WHAT YOU KNOW… About Credit Aplications (p.71)
Answers will vary. Students should check each other's work.

ACTIVITY 13—Applying for a Loan (p. 74)
Information on application will vary.

ACTIVITY 14—Completing Order Forms (p. 75)
Answers will vary. Have students exchange forms and check each other's
work.

ACTIVITY 15—Understanding Income Tax Words (p. 79)
If possible, have instruction booklets and forms for 1040EZ and 1040A
available in the classroom so students can practice filling out their own
returns.
1. D
2. I
3. A
4. J
5. C
6. F
7. E
8. G
9. H
10. B

ACTIVITY 16—Working with Income Tax Words (p. 79)
return; wages; interest; adjusted gross income; dependent; withheld; tax
table; refund

ACTIVITY 17—Using a 1040EZ (p. 80)
1. yes
2. $2000
3. $50
4. yes
5. yes
6. line 8

ACTIVITY 18—Working with Income Tax Words (p. 83)
joint return; dependent; exemptions; interest; dividends; tax-exempt;
unemployment compensation; IRA; withheld; refund

ACTIVITY 19—Using 1040A (p. 84)
1. yes
2. Married filing joint return (or 2)
3. yes
4. dependent son
5. 3
6. $48,899
7. $180
8. yes
9. line 9
10. yes
11. no
12. no
13. yes
14. that is the amount allowed for one exemption on 6e
15. $35,999
16. yes
17. 27
18. 28a
19. no
20. yes

Check Your Understanding of Tax Forms (p. 87)
(Numbers 1–8 below refer to line numbers on Form 1040EZ—1992—
shown in the student text.)

Alexander	1.	2,350	
	2.	36	
	3.	2,386	
	4.	yes	2,350
	5.	36	
	6.	72	
	7.	6	
	8.	66	
Fletcher	1.	11,020	
	2.	380	
	3.	11,400	
	4.	no	5,900
	5.	5,500	
	6.	975	
	7.	829	
	8.	146	

You may wish to have students work on blank 1040EZ forms available at
your local IRS office, complete with the worksheet on the back.